Alice Elizabeth Randall

The sources of Spenser's classical mythology

Alice Elizabeth Randall

The sources of Spenser's classical mythology

ISBN/EAN: 9783337057114

Printed in Europe, USA, Canada, Australia, Japan

Cover: Foto ©Thomas Meinert / pixelio.de

More available books at **www.hansebooks.com**

THE SOURCES

OF

SPENSER'S

CLASSICAL MYTHOLOGY

BY
ALICE ELIZABETH SAWTELLE (RANDALL), PH.D. (YALE)

SILVER, BURDETT AND COMPANY
NEW YORK . . . BOSTON . . . CHICAGO
1896

COPYRIGHT, 1896,
BY SILVER, BURDETT AND COMPANY.

TYPOGRAPHY BY C. J. PETERS & SON, BOSTON.
PRESSWORK BY BERWICK & SMITH.

TO
Professor Albert S. Cook.

PREFATORY NOTE.

Miss SAWTELLE's book was undertaken as a doctoral thesis in the English department of Yale University. It has been wrought out with singular care, and very little has been taken at second hand, so that it may fairly be depended upon as accurate in scholarship.

There ought, I should think, to be a modest place in colleges and schools for a work of this nature; certainly where Spenser is studied, and perhaps where attention is paid to any of the poetic Elizabethans. Spenser's mythology is by no means peculiar to himself, and much of it may be used for the illustration of poetry in its whole range from the times of great Elizabeth to the present.

Mr. Churton Collins, as well as Matthew Arnold, has made himself the spokesman of the doctrine that English literature should be studied in the light of the ancient classics; and perhaps this opuscule will be accepted by those who are of the same mind with these writers, as an illustration of their theory.

The author has necessarily traveled much in the realms of gold, while in quest of the materials for freighting her little craft; and I trust that her venture will do something to convince those who have doubted whether scholarship was quite compatible with literary appreciation, that the two need not perforce be disjoined.

A. S. C.

NEW HAVEN, *July*, 1896.

INTRODUCTION.

To the serious student no great author is an isolated fact, but rather the product of numerous influences, more or less direct. To see each author in his proper setting, not in relation to his own age only, but also to "those divine men of old time," is the aim of all worthy literary study; for then, and then only, can he be fully understood.

The unity of the great world-literature cannot be too early or too often insisted upon; and proud as we may be of the individual traits in our own English literature, it is, after all, strongly marked by foreign influences, ancient and modern. A thorough study of any one of its departments but confirms this view: the model of Milton's epic is to be found in Virgil's *Æneid*, and the *Iliad* and *Odyssey* of Homer; our lyrics are in many ways but the echoes of those sung many centuries ago by the shores of the Ægean Sea; and independent as was the growth of our drama on its romantic side, it has yet other, classical qualities, which find their source in the plays of Sophocles and Euripides.

After the Renaissance, which flooded England with originals and translations of ancient masterpieces, the classical note became a dominant one in our literature, and particularly did the richly imaginative mythology of Greece and Rome appeal to our poets.

No more conspicuous example of this fact can be cited than Edmund Spenser: the gods and heroes of antiquity glide over his pages as naturally as over those of Homer and Pindar, Virgil and Ovid. Mingled with the poet's own conceptions is a great mass of classical mythology; and it is the sources of this which are considered in this volume.

So far as is known, this is the first attempt that has been

made to furnish anything like a full treatment of Spenser's classical mythology, although fragmentary considerations of the subject have appeared from time to time. Such are those in Jortin's and Warton's *Remarks on Spenser;* but these essays — most excellent and suggestive as far as they go — are confessedly incomplete, for both scholars realized the extent of the subject touched upon. Furthermore, the sources of Spenser's mythology are treated in the notes of various editions of his works — notably those of Todd and Upton; but here, too, the treatment does not assume to be more than fragmentary, and there is certainly little attempt at grouping the various passages and comparing Spenser with himself.

An investigation conducted along these lines reveals some interesting facts in regard to Spenser's treatment of the classical myths, most conspicuous of which is his complete mastery of them. Never does he give us the impression that he is subservient to them, but always that they are at his bidding to help in carrying out the purposes of his poems. This sense of mastery leads him occasionally to rise superior to the strict letter of the original, and, while always preserving its spirit, he at times deliberately perverts a myth in order that it may better accord with his immediate purpose (see **Coronis**); or, again, he seizes upon some hint from the classics, and constructs a myth of his own, but so imbued with the spirit of its antique models that an expert might find it hard to detect the difference (see **Asteria**). Even when Spenser paraphrases long extracts from the classics, he embellishes them with beauties from his own imagination, so that he does not seem under limitations, even here (see **Arachne**).

Occasionally, however, our poet nods; and, either from carelessness or ignorance, makes mistakes in certain minor details (see **Palici**); but when we contemplate the vast extent of his borrowings from the classics, we can only wonder that these errors are not more numerous.

It is true that Spenser may be studied upon many sides; but no other view of him could impress one more deeply with the thoroughness of his scholarship. Although in certain minor details he may have been indebted to intermediate authorities, like

Natalis Comes (Noël Conti) — a popular mythographer of the sixteenth century — or to other poets of the Middle Ages, yet there is every evidence, from the paraphrasing of the Greek and Latin, and from the vital, original spirit breathing through the mythological passages, that he drew his inspiration directly from the fountain-heads. The numerous classical authorities cited by E. K. in support of the *Shepheard's Calender* would alone indicate this. Then, too, the catholicity of his knowledge must impress one. Although fascinated by Ovid, and under the spell of Virgil, he is inspired none the less by the Greek authors, from Homer and Hesiod down to Theocritus and Bion.

As Aubrey de Vere so aptly expresses it, "In one respect, however, it must be admitted that the Renaissance had assisted Spenser: it had imparted to him an acquaintance with classical, and especially with mythological lore, such as no mediæval writer possessed. His own profound sense of beauty made him fully appreciate what was thus presented to him; and whereas mediæval writers had often dealt with antiquity as mediæval painters had done, placing the head of a saint on the neck of a Hebe or a Mars, he entered into the spirit in an ampler manner than any of his predecessors, or than any southern poet." (*Characteristics of Spenser's Poetry*, Grosart Edition of Spenser.)

Occasional quotations have been made in the pages following from English translations of the classics: from the *Iliad*, translated by Lang, Leaf, and Myers; Butcher and Lang's *Odyssey*; the *Homeric Hymns*, translated by Parnell, Chapman, Shelley, Congreve, and Hole; Cooke's *Hesiod*; Myers' *Pindar*; Lawton's and Potter's *Euripides*; Taylor's *Greece of Pausanias*; Fawkes' *Apollonius Rhodius*; *Apuleius* (Bohn Library); Lonsdale and Lee's *Æneid*; Riley's *Ovid*; De Vere's *Horace*.

Acknowledgment is due also to Jortin's and Warton's *Remarks on Spenser* and Upton's and Todd's editions of Spenser, for ultimate help in the case of several difficulties already wrestled with, while it has been a pleasure to discover their confirmation of various particulars independently treated.

The Globe Edition of the Complete Works of Edmund Spenser has been used as the basis of this investigation; and its order and numbering have been followed, except in the case of

Virgil's Gnat, the references to which are to stanzas rather than to single verses.

The spelling of the proper names in the headings has been normalized to correspond to the usual Latin forms; and only when Spenser's spelling is so widely at variance with this as to cause possible confusion, has it been taken into account.

A. E. S.

YALE UNIVERSITY, *June,* 1896.

INDEX OF ABBREVIATIONS.

A. A. Ars Amatoria.
Æn. Æneid.
Am. Amoretti.
Amor. Amores.
Anac. Anacreon.
Anth. Lat. Anthologia Latina.
Apoll. Apollodorus.
Ap. Rh. Apollonius Rhodius.
Argonaut. Argonautica.
Aristoph. Aristophanes.
Ast. Astrophel.

Call. Callimachus.
Carm. Carmina.
Cic. Cicero.
Claud. Claudian.
Co. Cl. Colin Clout's Come Home Again.
Com. Commentarius ex Cicerone in Somnium Scipionis.

Daph. Daphnaida.
De Benef. De Beneficiis.
De. Nat. Deor. De Natura **Deorum**.
De Fluv. De Fluviis.
Dial. Deor. Dialogi Deorum.
Dial. Mort. Dialogi Mortuorum.
Diod. Sic. Diodorus Siculus.

Ecl. Eclogues.
Elec. Electra.
Ep. Epithalamion.
Eurip. Euripides.

Fab. Fables.
Fast. Fasti.
F. Q. Faerie Queene.

Georg. Georgics.
Gigant. Gigantomachia.

H. B. Hymne in Honour of Beautie.
Her. Heroides.
H. H. B. Hymne of Heavenly Beautie.
Hip. Hippolytus.
H. L. Hymne in Honour of Love.
Hom. Hymn. Homeric Hymn.
Hor. Horace.
Hyg. Hyginus.

Il. Iliad.
Imag. Imagines.
Int. Introduction.

Lucret. Lucretius.
Lyc. Lycophron.
Lys. Lysistrata.

Mart. Martial.
Met. Metamorphoses.
M. H. T. Mother Hubberds Tale.
Min. Minos.
Mui. Muiopotmos.

Nupt. Pel. et Thet. Nuptials of Peleus and Thetis.

Od. Odyssey.
Olymp. Olympic.
Orest. **Orestes**.
Orph. Orpheus.
Ov. Ovid.

Paus. Pausanias.
Phæd. Phædrus.
Plat. Plato.
Plut. Plutarch.
Poet. Astron. Poeticon Astronomicon.
Pont. **Ep.** Pontic Epistles.
Pref. **Preface**.

Pro.	Prothalamion.	Theb.	Thebaid.
Prol.	Prologue.	Theoc.	Theocritus.
Pyth.	Pythian.	Theog.	Theogony.
		T. M.	Teares of the Muses.
R. R.	Ruines of Rome.	Trist.	Tristia.
R. T.	Ruines of Time.	Tzet.	Tzetzes.
Sat.	Saturnalia.	V. B.	Visions of Bellay.
S. C.	Shepheards Calender.	Ver.	Verses.
Schol.	Scholiast.	V. G.	Virgils Gnat.
Serv.	Servius.	Virg.	Virgil.
Silv.	Silvæ.	V. W. V.	Visions of the Worlds Vanitie.
Soph.	Sophocles.		
Stat.	Statius.		
Strab.	Strabo.	W. and D.	Works and Days.
Sup.	Supplices.		

THE SOURCES OF SPENSER'S CLASSICAL MYTHOLOGY.

ACHERON. — F. Q. 1, 5. 33.

One of the rivers in the Lower World, mentioned by Virgil (*Æn.* 6. 295).

ACHILLES. — F. Q. 3. 2. 25; V. G. 66; H. L. 233.

F. Q. 3. 2. 25 contains a reference to the famous armor of Achilles, which, according to *Il.* 18. 468 ff., Vulcan made for Achilles at the request of Thetis.

In *V. G.* 66 the oft-repeated story of the triumph of Achilles (Æacides) over Hector is referred to. With this compare *Il.* 22, where a lengthy description of the combat between the two heroes is related. Spenser (upon his own authority, since the statement does not occur in the original of *Virgil's Gnat*) says that Achilles dragged the body of Hector three times around Troy. The authority for this is not found in the *Iliad*, which says that Achilles bound the body of Hector to his chariot and dragged him to the Greek camp; but in *Æn.* 1. 483: "Thrice round Ilium's walls had Achilles dragged Hector, and now he was selling his lifeless body for gold." For the death of Achilles at the hands of Paris (*V. G.* 67), see *Il.* 22. 359.

The power of love over Achilles is mentioned in *H. L.* 233: —

> Achilles preassing through the Phrygian glaives.

This is a reference to Achilles' love for Patroclus, whose death spurred him on to the battle with the Trojans, which is described in *Il.* 19. 20, ff. The immediate source of the allusion is shown from the grouping to be the *Symposium* of Plato.

ACONTIUS.—F. Q. 2. 7. 55.

The romantic story of the love of Acontius for Cydippe and of the means by which he won her love is here cited. As in several other myths, it was an apple which played the important part. This fair youth, Acontius, saw the beautiful Cydippe worshiping in the temple of Diana. He succumbed to her charms at once, and wished to make her his wife. In order to accomplish this, he threw an apple at her feet. On it was inscribed the solemn vow, "I swear by Diana to marry Acontius." Cydippe, receiving the apple, read the words aloud. She threw the apple away, but all too late. Her vow had been heard and registered, and after various delays she was wedded to Acontius.

The myth forms the groundwork of *Her.* 20, 21, which are attributed to Ovid; it is the subject also of one of the epistles of Aristænetus.

ACTÆA.—F. Q. 4. 11. 50. See Nereids.

ADMETUS.—F. Q. 3. 11. 39. See Apollo.

ADONIS.

No passage in the works of Spenser more plainly reveals that teeming imagination which has given him the name of "the poet's poet," than that which describes the gardens of Adonis (*F. Q.* 3. 6. 29 ff.). Underlying the poetry of it there is also a deep philosophy, the discussion of which does not concern us here. The myth upon which this and other passages rest is variously related:—

Apollodorus (3. 14. 4) says that Adonis was the son of a certain Myrrha, who had neglected the worship of Venus, and had been, in punishment, cursed with an unnatural love for her own father. The Gods took pity upon Myrrha, and changed her into a tree (comp. *Met.* 10. 299 ff.). When Myrrha's child Adonis was born, Venus was charmed by his beauty, and intrusted him to the keeping of Proserpina; but Proserpina, also captivated by the boy, refused to give him up. The case was submitted to Jove, who decided that two-thirds of each year Adonis should divide between Venus in this world and Proserpina in the lower regions; the remaining third he should have to himself. Adonis, however, preferred to spend the time allotted to himself in the company of **Venus**. **It was some** time after this that Adonis was killed, while **hunting, by a** wild boar.

The **same story, with** variations, is related by other authors, such **as Hyginus, Ovid,** Theocritus, and Bion. Ovid (*Met.* 10. 731 ff.) adds that, after his death, Adonis was changed by Venus **into a flower;** and others say that after that event Venus enjoyed **the** society of her beloved Adonis for only a half of each year. Spenser, in imagination, transferred the story of the love of Venus and Adonis to a piece of tapestry —

<blockquote>A worke of rare device and wondrous wit.</blockquote>

F. Q. 3. 1. 34 ff.

The unlawful love of Myrrha is referred to in *F. Q.* 3. 2. 41.

But all this story was originally something more than a mere poetic fiction: there was in it the basis of the worship of Adonis, which **was brought** from Syria, through Asia Minor, into Greece. The alternating death and revival of Adonis seem to typify the decay **and revival** of vegetation. This idea was prominently brought **out in the** Adonia, or annual festivals **of Adonis**. We learn from the ancients that they lasted two days: **the first commemorated** the disappearance of Adonis; the second, **his return** to life. On this occasion earthen vessels, called the "**gardens of Adonis**," were **placed** as symbols before the temples **of Adonis**. In them were planted herbs, which were forced to quick **growth only to decay as rapidly** (Aristoph. *Lys.* 362; *Pax*, 410; Theoc. *Adon.*). Thus **the** term "garden of Adonis" became synonymous with "hot-box," **as in the** *Phædrus* of Plato, where Socrates asks if a wise man would be likely to **plant his** seed in a garden of Adonis, and not rather in soil where it would grow to life in a natural way. It is on this term that Spenser has seized; and we have the amplification of the idea back **of it** in the **famous** description of the Gardens of Adonis — "the first seminary **Of all things that are borne to live and dye** According to their **kinds**" (*F. Q.* 3. 6. 21 ff.). The idea which pervades the passage — the indestructibility **of** life, which appears again and again under new forms — is familiar **to** us from the Pythagorean doctrine of metempsychosis.

Moreover, Pliny (19. 9) says that **the gardens of the** Hesperides **and of Kings Adonis and** Alcinous **were famous** among the ancients; and Homer (*Od.* 7. 112 ff.) describes that of Alcinous — a description which it is evident Spenser had in mind.

There are further references to the Gardens of Adonis in *F. Q.* 2. 10. 71 and *Co. Cl.* 804.

ÆACIDES.—F. Q. 6. 10. 22. See Peleus.

ÆACIDES (Ajax and Achilles).—**V. G. 66.**

Ajax and Achilles are each appropriately referred to under this patronymic, since they were the descendants of Æacus. In this stanza and the preceding, where Ajax is called the son of Telamon, the single combat of Hector and Ajax, and the bravery of the latter in defending the Greek ships against the fire which, under the instigation of Hector, the Trojans were bringing against them, are referred to. For the first incident see *Il.* 7. 1 ff.; for the second see *Il.* 15. 718 ff. Compare *V. G.* 62.

With *V. G.* 67, which states that Ulysses killed Ajax, compare Hyg. *Fab.* 107, according to which, Ajax killed himself when the arms of Achilles were awarded to Ulysses. For Æacides as name of Achilles, see **Achilles.**

ÆACUS.—V. G. 61.

Æacus is here mentioned as the father of Peleus and Telamon, and as the judge of the Lower World. Compare *Il.* 16. 15; *Met.* 13. 25 ff.

ÆGIDE (shield).—**Mui. 321.**

This is the Ægis, or shield of Jove, which was an attribute of his daughter Pallas also. It is described in *Il.* 5. 738 ff., as "the tasselled ægis terrible, whereon is Panic as a crown all round about; and Strife is therein and Valour and horrible Onslaught withal; and therein is the dreadful monster's Gorgon head, dreadful and grim, portent of ægis-bearing Zeus." It is to be noticed that, at this point, Pallas appropriates this shield, with the other armor of her father.

In *Æn.* 8. 435 ff., the ægis is described as "the armour of angry Pallas, with serpent-scales and gold, and the twine of snakes, and on the breast of the goddess the Gorgon's self, with eyes still rolling in her severed head." Compare *F. Q.* 3. 9. 22. See also *Met.* 6. 79.

ÆGINA. — F. Q. 3. 11. 35.

When Spenser makes the statement that **Jove** won Ægina in the form of fire, he is supported by *Met.* 6. 113. Both Apollorus (3. 12. 6) and Hyginus (*Fab.* 52) mention the union of Ægina and Jove. Though neither speaks of the metamorphosis, Apollodorus says that when Asopus, the father of Ægina, attempted to pursue Jove when he was escaping with Ægina, the Thunderer struck him with lightning.

ÆGERIA. — F. Q. 2. 10. 42.

Ægeria is here mentioned as a fay who taught Numa. With this compare Ov. *Fast.* 3. 263 and 275.

ÆNEAS. — F. Q. 3. 9. 40; H. L. 232.

The first of these passages is an outline of the story of the *Æneid*. The sacking of Troy; the escape of Æneas with his band of followers; his subsequent wanderings; the arrival in Latium, followed by wars; the founding of Alba Longa by Iulus, and that of Rome by Romulus, — all these points are touched upon.

ÆOLUS. — F. Q. 1. 7. 9; 3. 6. 44; 3. 11. 42; 4. 9. 23; Mui. 420.

Our poet, as he wrote these passages, must have had in mind those lines from the *Odyssey* (10. 1 ff.) where Æolus is described as the heaven-appointed lord of the winds, or that more familiar passage in the *Æneid* (1. 52 ff.) in which the winds are described as shut up in caves and restrained by the weight of mountains. They chafe under their confinement; but only at the bidding of Æolus, their ruler, may they go forth over land and sea.

In keeping with these accounts is the " blustring Æolus " of the first passage from Spenser, and the " sharp blast " of Æolus mentioned in the second, as is also the " gate " of Æolus in *Mui.* 420.

In making Æolus the father of Arne (*F. Q.* 3. 11. 42; 4. 9. 23), Spenser follows *Met.* 6. 115 and Diod. Sic. 4. 67. The picture of Æolus as an irate father, raving over the elopement of his daughter, is, in the fact of the rage, quite in keeping with life itself, while the manner in which the rage is exhibited is consistent with classical mythology.

ÆSCULAPIUS.—F. Q. 1. 5. 36; 1. 5. 39; 1. 5. 41. See Apollo and Hippolytus.

ÆSON.—R. R. 10. See Argonautic Expedition.

AGAMEMNON.—V. G. 69.

Since Agamemnon was the chief commander of the Greek forces in the Trojan War, even though not their hero, he is appropriately referred to here. See *Iliad, passim.*

For his relation to Tantalus, see **Tantalus.**

AGAVE.—F. Q. 4. 11. 49. See Nereids.

AGAVE.—V. G. 22. See Bacchus.

AGENOR.—F. Q. 4. 11. 15. See Founders of Nations.

AGLAIA.—F. Q. 6. 10. 22. See Graces.

ALBION.—F. Q. 2. 10. 11; 4. 11. 16. See Founders of **Nations.**

ALCESTIS.—V. G. 54.

Compare Eurip. *Alcestis,* where the incident here referred to is enlarged upon.

ALCIDES.—F. Q. 1. 7. 17; 2. 5. 31; 3. 12. 7; 4. 1. 23; 5. 8. 31; 6. 12. 32; Mui. 71. See Hercules.

ALCMENA.—F. Q. 3. 11. 33; R. T. 380; M. H. T. 1299; Ep. 328.

Spenser follows *Met.* 6. 112 when he mentions the affair with Alcmena among the amours of Jove; but when he says that Jove put three nights in one for her sake, he differs from Ovid, who says it was two nights (*Amor.* 1. 13. 45). Hyginus, also, says two nights (*Fab.* 29). Orpheus, on the other hand, says that on the occasion of this amour the sun did not shine for three days (*Argonaut.* 118). Apollodorus (2. 3. 8) also says the same. Spenser, then, may have been indebted to one of these for his statement, or to Lucian (*Dial. Deor.* 10).

Spenser further states that Mercury, with his caduceus, brought about this lengthened night. See **Mercury.**

ALEBIUS.—F. Q. 4. 11. 14. See Sea-Gods.

ALIMEDA.—F. Q. 4. 11. 51. See Nereids.

AMAZON.—F. Q. 2. 3. 31.

This is a reference to the queen of the Amazons, Penthesilea, who came to the assistance of Priam in the Trojan War.

In *Æn.* 1. 491 ff., we have a graphic picture of Penthesilea at the head of her troops of Amazons. Servius, commenting upon this passage, says that she was killed by Achilles, and this was the commonly accepted account of her death. Spenser, however, says she was slain by Pyrrhus, thus following Dares Phrygius, 36.

In the numerous passages of the fifth book of the *Faerie Queene* where the name "Amazon" occurs, it is freely used to designate a character of the poem whose warlike nature and deeds are patterned after the classical conception of the warlike Amazons.

F. Q. 4. 11. 21 derives the name of the River Amazon from a race of maiden warriors who possess it. This is in keeping with the story that the discoverer of that river named it Amazon because he saw some armed women on its banks.

AMMON.—F. Q. 1. 5. 48. See Jove.

AMPHION.—B. R. 25.

Amphion's instrument, here mentioned, is the golden shell whose music raised the walls of Thebes. See Apoll. 3. 5. 5, also Ap. Rh. 1. 740:—

> Behind, Amphion tuned his golden shell,
> Amphion, deem'd in music to excel:
> Rocks still pursued him as he moved along,
> Charm'd by the music of his magic song.

AMPHITRITE.

> Fair Amphitrite, most divinely faire,
> Whose yvorie shoulders weren covered all
> As with a robe, with her owne silver haire,
> And deckt with pearles which th' Indian seas for her prepaire.
> *F. Q.* 4. 11. 11.

In *Theog.* 930 she is mentioned as the wife of Neptune, and in the *Hom. Hymn to Apollo* (*Delian*) she is enumerated among the supreme goddesses of heaven who were present at the birth of Apollo.

In *F. Q.* 4. 11. 49 she appears simply as one of the Nereids. See Nereids.

She was a favorite subject with ancient artists, who delighted to linger over her beauties, as our poet does in the lines above quoted.

AMPHITRYONIDES.—F. Q. 7. 7. 36. See Hercules.

ANCHISES.—F. Q. 3. 9. 41. See Venus.

ANDROMEDA.—R. T. 649.

The peril from which Perseus freed Andromeda forms the subject of one of the favorite myths of antiquity. Apollodorus (2. 3. 3) relates that Cassiopea, the mother of Andromeda, boasted that her beauty surpassed that of the Nereids. In return for this presumption, Neptune caused the land to be flooded, and sent a sea-monster which terrified the people. According to an oracle, there was no escape from these calamities unless Andromeda should be exposed to the monster. Her father, Cepheus, was obliged to conform to the demands of his people; and, accordingly, Andromeda was chained to a rock. It is at this point that Perseus came to her release.

This story is related by Ovid (*Met.* 4. 663 ff.) and by Hyginus (*Fab.* 64). It is worth noting that Hyginus says that it was the beauty of Andromeda of which her mother boasted. This would make the punishment of the innocent girl somewhat more reasonable.

For the statement that Perseus, when he freed Andromeda, was mounted on the winged steed Pegasus, there is no classical authority. Since, however, he was equipped with wings on this occasion, and released Andromeda just after killing Medusa, the confusion is quite explicable.

ANTIOPE.—F. Q. 3. 11. 35.

> In Satyres shape Antiopa he snatcht.

Compare this statement with *Met.* 6. 110; also with Apoll. 3. 5. 5.

AON.—F. Q. 4. 11. 15. See Founders of Nations.

APOLLO.

There is a reference to the parentage of Apollo in *V. G.* 2. He is there spoken of as —

> The golden offspring of Latona pure,
> And ornament of Jove's great progenie.

F. Q. 6. 2. 25 also refers to him as the son of Latona. Such was the commonly accepted belief among the ancients, in support of which may be cited *Theog.* 918.

The well-known story which relates the anger of Juno and the escape of Latona to the Isle of Delos, where she gave birth to Apollo and his twin sister Artemis, is outlined in *F. Q.* 2. 12. 13. This may be founded upon the *Hom. Hymn to Apollo* (Delian), or upon later versions of the same story, such as Apoll. 1. 4. 1 and Hyg. *Fab.* 140.

Apollo is mentioned as the father of various children: of Æsculapius (*F. Q.* 1. 5. 43); of Phaeton (*F. Q.* 1. 4. 9; *T. M.* 7); of Pæon, by Liagore (*F. Q.* 3. 4. 41); of the Muses, by Memory (*F. Q.* 1. 11. 5; 3. 3. 4); of the Muses without reference to Memory (*T. M.* 2; *Ep.* 121).

Many ancient writers agree in making Apollo the father of Æsculapius by Coronis, as, for instance, Pindar (*Pyth.* 3); Euripides (*Alcestis*, Prol.); Hyginus (*Fab.* 202); Ovid (*Met.* 2. 9).

There does not seem to be the same agreement among the ancients in regard to Apollo's relation to Phaeton; but, in making him his father, Spenser is amply supported by such writers as Ovid (*Met.* 2. 1 ff.) and Hyginus (*Fab.* 152).

In Spenser's reference to Apollo as the father of Pæon by Liagore, we have an instance of the liberty which Spenser sometimes takes with classical mythology. The passage in question is as follows: —

> This Liagore whilome had learned skill
> In leaches craft, by great Apolloes lore,
> Sith her whilome upon high Pindus hill
> He loved, and at last her wombe did fill
> With hevenly seed, whereof wise Pæon sprong.
> *F. Q.* 3. 4. 41.

Now, Liagore is nowhere mentioned by ancient writers, except by Hesiod in the *Theogony*, where she is cited as one of the Nereids; and Spenser also mentions her in his list (*F. Q.* 4. 11. 51). It is evident that our poet is thinking of Œnone, the wife of Paris, whom Apollo loved, and to whom he taught the art of healing (see *Her.* 5. 139). It is a question whether Spenser here regarded Pæon as a son distinct from Æsculapius, or whether he used the name for Æsculapius. Homer speaks of Pæon as physician of the gods (*Il.* 5. 401, 899) and as distinct from Æsculapius, but does not refer to him as the son of Apollo.

With many of the ancients, Pæon is simply a surname for Æsculapius or Apollo, indicating possession of the power to heal; but, as said before, they, for the most part, agree in making Æsculapius the son of Apollo by Coronis. Thus it is clear that, whichever view Spenser has in mind, he deviates from classical mythology.

For Apollo's relation to the Muses see **Muses**.

For Apollo's relation to the water divinities (*F. Q.* 4. 11. 52) see **Nereids**.

Apollo's love for various women is mentioned: for Climene (*F. Q.* 3. 11. 38); for Coronis (*F. Q.* 3. 11. 37); for Daphne (*F. Q.* 2. 12. 52; 3. 11. 36); for Issa (*F. Q.* 3. 11. 39). His affection for Hyacinthus also is cited in *F. Q.* 3. 11. 37. For all these see the several headings.

In *F. Q.* 3. 11. 39, after mentioning the above names of those who won the love of Phœbus, Spenser makes a general statement in regard to the transformations of Phœbus into a lion, a stag, and a falcon. This, with a slight difference, is copied from *Met.* 6. 122 ff.: "There was Phœbus, under the form of a rustic; and how, besides, he was wearing the wings of a hawk at one time, at another the skin of a lion."

Phœbus was primarily the god of the sun. Homer and other of the early Greek writers represent Phœbus and Helios as perfectly distinct, but in later times the two became identical. That Phœbus was the god of the sun — the giver of light and warmth and life to the earth — accounts for his numerous other attributes. He figures as the god of intellectual light, delighting in poetry and art, and in the foundation of cities and civil institutions; as the protector of flocks; as the god of prophecy, bringing hidden things to light; as the god of the healing art; and, again, as the hurler of death-dealing darts.

Again and again throughout his poems Spenser refers to Phœbus as the god of the sun. Sometimes he uses the name for the sun itself; sometimes he speaks of the "lamp" of Phœbus, or the "car" of Phœbus; and again, of his "golden face" or "golden head." See *F. Q.* 1. Int. 4; 1. 1. 23; 1. 2. 1; 1. 2. 29; 1. 5. 2; 1. 5. 20; 1. 5. 44; 1. 6. 6; 1. 7. 29; 1. 7. 34; 1. 11. 31; 1. 12. 2; 2. 8. 5; 2. 9. 10; 3. 2. 24; 3. 5. 27; 3. 6. 44; 3. 10. 1;

3. 10. 45; 5. 3. 19; 5. 11. 62; 6. 3. 29; 7. 6. 39; 7. 7. 51; *S. C.* Jan. 73; Apr. 73; Aug. 83; Oct. 3; Nov. 14; *V. G.* 21; 78; *V. W. V.* 2; *Ep.* 77.

As god of poets, Apollo appears at the wedding of Peleus and Thetis, singing the marriage hymn to the delight of the other gods (*F. Q.* 7. 7. 12). In mentioning this Spenser says, "They say." The "they" may be Homer (*Il.* 24. 62). There Juno says to Apollo:—

. . . and **thou** among them **wert** feasting with thy lyre.

Again this god of song essays a mightier theme — the triumphs of Phlegræan Jove (*F. Q.* 2. 10. 3). Statius (*Theb.* 6. 336) pictures Apollo upon the heights of heaven, charming the Muses with his song, the oft-repeated theme of which is Jove and Phlegra.

T. M. 330 likewise refers to Apollo's famous "quill."

The musical contest between Apollo and Pan is cited in *S. C.* June 68. Ovid (*Met.* 11. 146 ff.) relates the familiar story of the boastful challenge to Apollo on the part of Pan, and the rash preference of Midas for the rustic music of the latter. Such stupidity called down the anger of Apollo, and Midas bore henceforth the ears of the ass.

Apollo is not only the author of song, but the inspirer of it as well (*V. G.* 2, 7). From Homeric times down the bard was supposed to derive his inspiration from the Muses or from their leader, Apollo. Certain haunts of Apollo are mentioned in connection with the first of these references: Xanthus, the woods of Astery, Mt. Parnassus, Castalia, and the Pierian streams. The last three are especially distinguished as the haunts of the Muses, and, therefore, of Apollo. Horace (*Carm.* 4. 6.) bids Phœbus —

> Leave Lycian Xanthus who caresses
> With his soft wave thy golden tresses.

Asteria was, according to Apoll. 1. 4. 1, the original name of Delos, the birthplace of Apollo.

We have in this reference a hint of another one of Apollo's offices: Pales, the Roman god of shepherds, is called upon to attend Apollo. The belief that Apollo watched over flocks and cattle is a very early one. Homer (*Il.* 2. 766) says that Apollo fed the steeds of Eumelus in Pieria. It will be remembered also that it was the oxen of Apollo that the infant Mercury stole (*Hom. Hymn to Hermes*). But this idea is most familiarly embodied in the story of Apollo's caring for the flocks of Admetus, referred to by Spenser in *F. Q.* 3. 11. 39. According to Apoll. 3. 10. 4, Apollo was condemned to this service because he had killed the Cyclops, on account of their having furnished the thunderbolts with which Zeus destroyed Æsculapius. Euripides thus makes Apollo himself explain his position:—

> Home of Admetos, wherein I have borne
> To accept a menial's fare, although a god!
> Zeus was the cause, who slew Asclepios,
> My son, with lightnings hurled against his breast.
> Thereat of course enraged, I slew the Cyclops
> Who forged the holy flame; for this my sire
> In penance made me serve a mortal man.
> *Alcestis, Prol.*

F. Q. 2. 9. 48 contains a reference to Apollo as the god of prophecy, whose utterances were accepted as final:—

> Not he, whom Greece, the Nourse of all good arts,
> By Phœbus doome the wisest thought alive,
> Might be compar'd to these by many parts.

This surpassingly wise man is Socrates. In Plato's *Apologia* we read that Chærepho, an intimate associate of Socrates, went to the oracle at Delphi, and asked if there was any one more wise than Socrates; and the Pythian priestess replied that there was not.

There are several references to Apollo as physician (*F. Q.* 3. 4. 41; 4. 6. 1; 4. 12. 25). For this conception there is ample authority in classical mythology. As god of the sun, who sees all things, and as the god of prophecy, Apollo was looked upon as the divinity who averted evil. From this conception it was but a step to that of Apollo as physician, already alluded to in connection with Liagore above; and as such he was regarded as the father of Æsculapius, and as identical with Pæon.

But Apollo is not only the averter of evil, but also the god who punished evil-doers. As such he is possessed of deadly and unerring arrows. Spenser but follows Homer (*Il.* 1. 44 ff.) and numerous others among the ancients when he says: —

> But such as could both Phœbus arrowes ward
> And th' hayling darts of heaven beating hard.
> *Mui.* 79 ff.

In *F. Q.* 3. 6. 2 these "hayling darts" are viewed as "faire beams," and with them Phœbus adorned Venus, when, upon proceeding to Olympus, she delighted him and the other gods with her beauty (see *Hom. Minor Hymn to Aphrodite*).

In *V. G.* 84 we read that the laurel is "the ornament of Phœbus toil." How this tree came to be sacred to Apollo is related by Ovid (*Met.* 1. 12).

> The fierce Spumador, borne of heavenly seed
> Such as Laomedon of Phœbus race did breed.
> *F. Q.* 2. 11. 19.

This seems to be a somewhat tangled allusion to the myth that Apollo reared the horses of Eumelus Pheretiades in Pieria (*Il.* 1. 766) and to the story of his watching the cattle of Laomedon on Mt. Ida (*Il.* 21. 488).

In *F. Q.* 7. 6. 35 Spenser represents Apollo as the scribe of the gods, though upon what authority we cannot say.

ARACHNE. — F. Q. 2. 7. 28; 2. 12. 77; **Mui.** 261, etc.

The lengthy passage in *Muiopotmos* which relates the contest between Minerva and Arachne is evidently a translation of the same story as given by Ovid, *Met.* 6. 70 ff., as the following comparison will show: —

> Arachne figur'd how Jove did abuse
> Europa like a Bull, and on his backe
> Her through the sea did beare; so lively seene,
> That it true Sea, and true Bull, ye would weene.
> SPENSER.

> Mæonis elusam designat imagine tauri
> Europam: verum taurum, freta vera putares.
> OVID.

She seem'd still backe unto the land to **looke**,
And her play-fellowes aide to call, and feare
The dashing of the waves, that up she tooke
Her daintie feete, and garments gathered neare.
                                                    SPENSER.

Ipsa videbatur terras spectare relictas
Et comites clamare suas, tactumque vereri
Assilientis aquæ timidasque reducere plantas.
                                                    OVID.

Instead of giving **the list of the** loves **of Jupiter, Neptune,** Phœbus, Liber, and Saturn as enumerated **at this point by Ovid** (a passage of which Spenser makes use in another connection), Spenser says: —

Before the Bull she pictur'd winged Love, etc.

And round **about** her worke she did empale
With a faire border wrought of sundrie **flowres,**
Enwoven **with an** Yvie-winding trayle.
                                                    SPENSER.

Ultima pars **telæ tenui** circumdata **limbo**
Nexilibus flores **hederis** habet intertextos.
                                                    OVID.

A goodly worke, **full fit** for king**ly bowres;**
Such as Dame **Pallas,** such as Envie **pale,**
That al good **things** with venemous **tooth devowres,**
Could not **accuse.**
                                                    SPENSER.

Non illud **Pallas, non** illud carpere Livor
Possit opus.
                                                    OVID.

She made the storie of the **olde debate**
Which she with Neptune did **for Athens trie.**
                                                    SPENSER.

Cecropia Pallas scopulum **Mavortis in arce**
Pingit et antiquam de terræ nomine **litem.**
                                                    OVID.

Twelve gods doo **sit around** in royall state,
And Jove in midst with awfull Majestie,
To judge the strife betweene them stirred late.
                                                    SPENSER.

Bis **sex** cælestes medio Jove sedibus **altis**
Augusta gravitate sedent.
                                                    OVID.

Each of the Gods, by his like visnomie
Eathe to be knowen; but Jove above them all,
By his great lookes and power Imperiall.
SPENSER.

. . . sua quemque deorum
Inscribit facies. Jovis est regalis imago.
OVID.

Before them stands the God of Seas in place,
Clayming that sea-coast Citie as his right.
And strikes the rockes with his three-forked mace;
Whenceforth issues a warlike steed in sight,
The signe by which he chalengeth the place.
SPENSER.

Stare deum pelagi longoque ferire tridente
Aspera saxa facit, medioque e vulnere saxi
Exiluisse ferum; quo pignore vindicet urbem.
OVID.

Then to her selfe she gives her Ægide shield,
And steelhed speare, and morion on her hedd,
Such as she oft is seene in warlicke field;
Then sets she forth, how with her weapon dredd
She smote the ground, the which streight foorth did yield
A fruitfull Olyve tree, with berries spredd,
That all the Gods admir'd: then, all the storie
She compast with a wreathe of Olyves hoarie.
SPENSER.

At sibi dat clipeum, dat acutæ cuspidis hastam,
Dat galeam capiti; defenditur ægide pectus:
Percussamque sua simulat de cuspide terram
Edere cum bacis fetum canentis olivæ;
Mirarique deos: . . . .
. . . .
Circuit extremas oleis pacalibus oras.
OVID.

The dots of omission in this last quotation indicate the passage portraying the punishments of those who, like Arachne, had assumed a presumptuous attitude toward some divinity — a passage which Spenser omits, and in place of which, for the purposes of his poem, he describes a butterfly among the olives.

It should be noted also that Spenser inverts the two parts of the story as given by Ovid, placing the description of Arachne's work first.

ARGONAUTIC EXPEDITION.

The references which bear upon this general subject are as follows: To the Argo itself and the flower of Greece, which it bore; to the famous history of Jason and Medea, including her charms, her love for Jason, his conquest of the fleece, and his breach of faith (*F. Q.* 2. 12. 44). To the pine as ornament of the Argo (*V. G.* 27). To the quarrel among the Argonauts (*F. Q.* 4. 1. 23). To Hypsipyle (*F. Q.* 2. 10. 56). To the mishap of Hylas and the grief of Hercules over his loss (*F. Q.* 3. 12. 7). To Jason's sowing the dragon's teeth (*R. R.* 10). To the bones of her brother scattered by Medea upon the Colchic strand (*F. Q.* 5. 8. 47). To the murder of Creusa by Medea (*F. Q.* 2. 12. 45).

There are a number of more or less detailed accounts of the Argonautic Expedition among the ancient classics. Such are those of Pindar (*Pyth.* 4); of Orpheus (*Argonaut.*); of Apollodorus (1. 9); of Apollonius Rhodius (*Argonaut.*); and of Ovid (*Met.* 7. 1 ff, and *Trist.* 3. 9).

Pindar's treatment of the subject is too general to have furnished Spenser with the points above mentioned.

Orpheus gives the list of heroes who went on the Argo; he further describes the "mighty charms" by which the fleece was at last won, and the love of Medea for Jason. He mentions, besides, the adventure of the Argonauts on the isle of Lemnos, where they charmed the Amazons, who inhabited it, — among them their queen, Hypsipyle; also the loss of Hylas, who was stolen by a water-nymph. Orpheus further relates the crime of Medea in killing her brother Absyrtus: he says that he was thrown down the banks of a river and borne on its current to the sea, and the islands where the bones were afterwards washed up were named for him — *Absyrtides.*

Apollodorus furnishes all the details mentioned by Spenser except the quarrel. He says that Medea killed her brother, and tore him limb from limb; that her father collected his bones, and buried them at a place afterwards called *Tomi* in memory of the deed.

Apollonius Rhodius has left us a story of the Argonautic Expedition, extending through four books. In the first book we have a list of the heroes, whom Spenser designates as "the flowr of Greece." There is an account, too, of the quarrel between the chiefs, which occurred before the Argo sailed, and was ended by the intervention of Orpheus. Hypsipyle and Hylas both are mentioned. In the third book Medea's charms are dwelt upon, and "her furious loving fit." The fourth book is concerned with the conquest of the fleece, and the adventures of the Argonauts on their return voyage to Greece.

There are scattered references to the pine of which the Argo was built, with which may be compared *V. G.* 27, where it is called the ornament of the Argo. The subsequent fickleness of Jason is not referred to. In regard to the murder of Medea's brother, Apollonius Rhodius says it took place upon one of the Brugi, and at the hands of Jason, Medea being an accomplice in the deed. There is, however, no mention of the scattering of the bones.

Ovid (*Trist.* 3. 9) speaks of the Argo as the first ship to speed through waves before untried. He then goes on to describe the killing of Absyrtus by Medea. He says she scattered her brother's bones about the fields. The place of the murder was Tomi.

In *Met.* 7. 1 ff., the story of the Argonauts is taken up at the point of the arrival in Colchis; the references, then, which Spenser makes to occurrences before that event are omitted. From the arrival to the murder of her sons by Medea, Ovid gives a detailed account of "the famous history."

It will be seen, then, that from no one of these accounts could Spenser have drawn, but rather from an amalgamation of several different ones.

Numerous single passages might be quoted to prove that Jason was the son of Æson, as stated in R. R. 10.

Yt seemd thenchaunted flame which did Creusa wed.
F. Q. 2. 12. 45.

Creusa (or Glauce) was the woman for whom Jason abandoned Medea. This particular reference is explained in the light of Apollodorus 1. 9. 28: Medea avenged herself by sending Creusa a robe permeated with poison of a combustible nature. When Creusa put the garment on she perished in flames.

ARGUS.

Spenser's allusions to Argus are very slight. They may be classed under two heads: those which pertain to his numerous eyes, as *F. Q.* 3. 9. 7; *S. C.* Jul. 154; Sept. 203; and those which refer to the myth that those eyes were placed in the tail of the peacock, as *F. Q.* 1. 4. 17 and *S. C.* Oct. 32.

Apollodorus (2. 1. 2) says that the surname of Argus was Panoptes, and that he had eyes in his whole body. He relates, further, that he was chosen by Juno to guard Io, whom Jupiter had transformed into a cow; but, though he mentions the fact that Argus was killed by Mercury, he does not say that Juno placed his numerous eyes in the tail of her own bird. In Ovid, however (*Met.* 1. 601 ff.), we have this myth in greater detail. We read that "Argus had his head encircled with a hundred eyes," and that later "the daughter of Saturn takes them and places them on the feathers of her own bird, and she fills its tail with starry gems."

ARIADNE.

> Looke! how the crowne which Ariadne wore
> Upon her yvory forehead, that same day
> That Theseus her unto his bridale bore
> When the bold Centaures made that bloudy fray,
> With the fierce Lapithes which did them dismay,
> Being now placed in the firmament,
> Through the bright heaven doth her beames display,
> And is unto the starres an ornament,
> Which round about her move in order excellent.
> *F. Q.* 6. 10. 13.

There is one point in which the mythology of this passage is not accurate: the quarrel between the Lapithæ and the Centaurs did not occur at the marriage of Theseus and Ariadne, but at the nuptials of Pirithous, whose "feare" Spenser elsewhere calls Theseus. (See *Met.* 12. 210 ff.).

In regard to the crown of Ariadne, Spenser follows but one of several myths in making it the gift of Theseus to Ariadne upon their wedding-day. Hyginus (*Poet. Astron.* 2. Corona) has a long discussion on this point; while some writers say that the crown was given to Ariadne by Venus, at her wedding with Bacchus, there is authority for making it the gift of Theseus at his marriage with Ariadne. All writers, however, agree that it was Bacchus who placed the crown among the stars (see *Met.* 8. 177 ff.).

ARION.

The beautiful myth of Arion's charming the dolphin by the power of his music is related at some length by Ovid (*Fast.* 2. 83 ff.). He tells how the tuneful Arion found himself in the hands of a merciless crew on board a vessel; how escape seemed impossible, till, seizing his lyre, he leaped into the water, and, by the aid of his music, pressed a dolphin into his service; and how, borne upon the back of the dolphin, he glided over the waves to safety. Spenser abridges the myth to the compass of a few lines (*F. Q.* 4. 11. 23), and in *Am.* 38 he employs it in skillful comparison.

ARNE. — F. Q. 3. 11. 42.

The statement that Neptune turned himself into a steer in order to beguile Arne, the daughter of Æolus, is founded upon *Met.* 6. 115. See also Diod. Sic. 4. 67.

ASOPUS. — F. Q. 4. 11. 14. See Sea-Gods.

ASTERIA. — F. Q. 3. 11. 34.

Like the foregoing amours of Jove, this is taken from Ovid's list (*Met.* 6. 108). With it compare Apoll. 1. 4. 1.

ASTERIA. — Mui. 119, etc. See Venus.

ASTRÆA. — F. Q. 5. 1. 5. Daph. 218.

We have in Astræa, as here pictured, the ideal of justice dwelling among men in some far-off time before the race fell from its perfect state. Hyginus (*Poet. Astron.* 2. Virgo), quoting Aratus, says that Astræa lived in the golden age of peace and plenty. When, however, justice declined, she could not endure the state of affairs, and so left the earth for the sky.

ASTRÆUS. — F. Q. 4. 11. 13. See Sea-Gods.

ATALANTA. — F. Q. 2. 7. 54. Am. 77.

Both of these passages refer to the apples by means of which Atalanta was outrun, the first mentioning the fact that it was a

Eubœan youth who resorted to the strategy, and thus succeeded in outstripping the swift-footed Atalanta.

This story is related by both Apollodorus (3. 9. 2) and Ovid (*Met.* 10. 560 ff.), but with the difference that, according to Apollodorus, the name of the successful youth was Melanion, while, with Ovid, it is Hippomenes. Spenser employs neither name, but, as mentioned above, calls the successful competitor "the Eubœan young man." This would indicate that he took the story from Apollodorus rather than from Ovid; for, according to Apollodorus, Melanion was the son of a certain Amphidamas, and we are told by Hesiod (*W. and D.* 654) that Amphidamas was a king of Chalcis, on the island of Eubœa. Thus Spenser might properly speak of his son as "the Eubœan young man."

ATE. — F. Q. 2. 7. 55; 4. 1. 19; 4. 1. 47; 4. 2. 11; 4. 4. 10; 4. 4. 11; 4. 5. 22; 4. 5. 31; 4. 9. 24; 5. 9. 47.

It is evident that Spenser makes Ate identical with Eris, because he says (*F. Q.* 2. 7. 55) that it was Ate who threw the apple among the gods: —

> For which th' Idæan Ladies disagreed,
> Till partiall Paris dempt it Venus dew,
> And had of her fayre Helen for his meed,
> That many noble Greekes and Trojans made to bleed,

and in *F. Q.* 4. 1. 22, he hints the same. According to the ancients, however, it was Eris who stirred that fatal strife (see Hyg. *Fab.* 92).

But there is no essential difference in the character of the two. They are both divinities delighting in discord and strife.

According to Homer, Ate was the daughter of Jove, once inhabiting Olympus, but banished thence because she had dared to outwit Jove himself (*Il.* 19. 128); but Hesiod (*Theog.* 230) says she was the daughter of Eris, who, in turn, was the daughter of Night, who was born of Chaos. Such an ancestry would warrant Spenser in saying (*F. Q.* 4. 1. 26) that Ate was " borne of hellish brood," and would, indeed, furnish him with a suggestion for that marvelous allegorical picture of the "mother of debate" and her abode which he draws at length in *F. Q.* 4. 1. 19 ff. What but the imagination of Spenser could have produced that image of her foul face, squinted eyes, **loathly** mouth; of her divided tongue and heart; her distorted ears; her feet unlike, **and** pointed in opposite directions; **her hands** interfering with each other? Almost as striking is the description of her abode, "Hard by the gates of hell . . . With thornes and barren brakes environd round."

Homer very appropriately calls Ate " venerable," and Spenser likewise (*F. Q.* 5. 9. 47) speaks of her as "that old hag."

ATLAS.— F. Q. 2. 7. 54; 3. 1. 57; Ver. 2.

The first of these passages refers to Atlas as the father of the Hesperides; the second refers to him as the father of the Hyades; the third, to the myth which represents Atlas as sustaining the firmament upon his shoulders. There is ample support for all in the ancient mythology. Not that Spenser calls the daughters of Atlas by name: the Hesperides he alludes to as those who were conquered by Hercules in their guardianship over the golden apples; the Hyades, as the " moist daughters."

Ancient authorities by no means agree as to the parentage of the Hesperides; but Spenser has the support of Diodorus Siculus (4. 27) in calling them the daughters of Atlas. They were appointed by Juno to guard upon Mt. Atlas the apples which she had received at her marriage; but the eleventh labor imposed upon Hercules was to obtain these apples. This he did by the assistance of Atlas. For the ancient authorities on this point see Hercules.

There is the same disagreement among the ancients as to the parentage of the Hyades. Spenser follows Ovid (*Fast.* 3. 105; 5. 169) in calling Atlas their father.

Servius, in commenting upon *Æn.* 1. 744, mentions, among other alleged derivations of the name Hyades, that from the Greek verb ὕεν, *to rain* — a derivation based upon the belief that the rising of the Hyades produced rain. Thus Virgil calls them "the rainy Hyades" (*Æn.* 1. 744; 3. 516); Horace speaks of their sad portent (*Carm.* 1. 3); and Spenser, following these poets, calls the Hyades "moist" (*F. Q.* 3. 1. 57).

The setting of the Hyades is poetically described by Spenser thus: —

> And the moist daughters of huge Atlas **strove**,
> Into the Ocean deepe to drive their weary drove.
> *F. Q.* 3. 1. 57.

Such passages as *Il.* 18. 489 might be cited as having suggested to Spenser the disappearance of the Hyades into the **ocean** — ". . . and [the Bear] alone hath no part in the baths of the ocean;" or the similar passage in *Georg.* 1. 246; or *Met.* 15. 30 — "Candidus Oceano nitidum Caput abdiderat Sol." Their "drove," of which Spenser speaks above, may possibly have been suggested by the "grege" in *Fast.* 5. 164.

ATROPOS. — F. Q. 4. 2. 48; 4. 2. 49. See Fates.

AURORA. — F. Q. 1. 4. 16; 1. 11. 51; 3. 10. 1; 3. 3. 20; V. G. 9.

The goddess of dawn appears so often upon the pages of the ancients that it would be difficult to say just where Spenser derived his passing references to her. In *F. Q.* 1. 4. 16 he described her as decked in "purple pall," and again (*F. Q.* 1. 11. 51) he speaks of her "rosy cheekes." The adjective "purpurea" is frequently used by the Latin poets to describe Aurora, but the different shades indicated by that word merge into one another like the colors of the dawning east: it may mean "purple" or "red" or "violet" or even "blackish." Thus, in *Met.* 3. 184, we read of "purpureæ Auroræ." The adjective "rosea" also is used by the poets in describing Aurora. (See Lucretius, 5. 655.) Thus also in *V. G.* 9 we read of her "rosy hair." "Rosea" may mean, not only "rose-colored," but also "of roses." Such passages as *Æn.* 7. 26, where Aurora is described as riding in her rosy (*roseus*) car, no doubt suggested to Spenser the "flower-decked chariot" of *F. Q.* 1. 11. 51.

"Crocea," also, is used in the classics as descriptive of Aurora: thus in *Æn.* 7. 25 she is described as "yellow morn," and Ovid (*Amor.* 2. 4. 43) speaks of how charming she is with her saffron locks. Spenser follows him when he describes her "golden locks" hanging loosely about her ears.

There are two references to her as the wife of the aged Tithonus (*F. Q.* 1. 11. 51; 3. 3. 20). The *Hom. Hymn to Venus* relates the story of Aurora's mistake in asking Jove that her husband might be immortal, and forgetting to ask for him also perpetual youth. With these two passages from Spenser compare the first lines of *Od.* 5: " Now the Dawn arose from her couch, from the side of the lordly Tithonus, to bear light to the immortals and to mortal men."

AUTONOE.— F. Q. 4. 11. 50. See Nereids.

AVERNUS.— F. Q. 1. 5. 31.

It is evident throughout this entire passage that Spenser had in mind the descent of Æneas into Hades (*Æn.* 6. 237 ff.). There Lake Avernus is represented as the entrance to Hell: "There was a cavern, deep and huge, with its vast mouth, craggy, sheltered by its black lake and forest gloom, o'er which no birds might speed along unharmed; such an exhalation, pouring from its black jaws, rose to the vault of heaven; wherefore the Greeks named the spot *Avernus.*"

BACCHUS.

Out of the great mass of tradition pertaining to Bacchus, Spenser has selected several points. As the god of wine, or, by metonymy, as wine itself, Bacchus is referred to in *F. Q.* 1. 6. 15; 2. 1. 55; 3. 9. 30. In *F. Q.* 5. 1. 2 we have a reference to him as the champion of justice. *T. M.* 461 is a declaration by Calliope, the muse of epic poetry, that she raised Bacchus to heaven. In *F. Q.* 5. 8. 47; *V. G.* 22 there are allusions to the tragic death of Pentheus, who was torn to pieces by his own mother, Agave, during some Bacchic orgies.

In the *Hom. Hymn to Bacchus*, which relates how Bacchus transformed the crew of a ship into dolphins, and the ship itself into a vine, Bacchus declares himself to be the raging god of wine — the son of Jove and Semele. The same myth is treated by Ovid (*Met.* 3. 631 ff.). In the *Iliad* and *Odyssey*, too, he figures as the god of wine.

Ep. 255 bids that Bacchus, as well as Hymen, be crowned at the marriage. Although it does not appear that the crowning of this god was a regular part of the marriage festival of the ancients, as was that of Hymen with the Romans, yet it is not inappropriate that the god of wine and revelry should be introduced here. Furthermore, in ancient art and literature the crown of vine-leaves and ivy is a noticeable feature of this god. See Horace, *Carm.* 3. 25; 4. 8.

It is a very interesting study to trace the development of the attributes of this divinity. In Homeric times he was the god of wine, who taught men the cultivation of the vine; this idea was further developed, until he became identified with the cultivation of trees and shrubs in general. Thus far he seems to be the personification of productive life in nature. In later times, however, this god of superabounding energy takes on a more ethical character, and becomes the champion of law and order. It is in this character that he appears in the following lines: —

> Such first was Bacchus, that with furious might,
> All th' East, before untam'd, did over-ronne,
> And wrong repressed, and establisht right,
> Which lawlesse men had formerly fordonne:
> There Justice first her princely rule begonne.
>
> *F. Q.* 5. 1. 2.

It was a common tradition that, as Hercules conquered the West, so Bacchus, accompanied by numerous raging attendants, swept through the East, especially India, introducing the cultivation of the vine, founding cities, and establishing laws. Apollodorus (3. 5. 2) mentions this, as do Diodorus Siculus (2. 38) and Ovid (*Fast.* 3. 720).

The conquests of Bacchus, like those of Hercules, were so vast as to be on an epic scale. Thus is it particularly appropriate that Calliope, the muse of epic poetry, should declare that it was she who had raised Bacchus and Hercules to heaven — that is, made them famous for all time (*T. M.* 461).

But woe unto the man who dared to oppose the cultivation of the vine and the introduction of the mad orgies which accompanied the mystic worship of Bacchus! Such a man was Pentheus, the son of the Bacchante Agave. Intruding in anger upon the sacred rites which were being celebrated upon Mt. Cithæron in Bœotia, his mother, in her frenzy, mistook him for a boar, and struck him with her thyrsus. Whereupon, she and her sister Bacchantes rushed upon the wretched Pentheus, and tore him limb from limb. Thus did he become an example of the foolishness of withstanding the worship of Bacchus (*Met.* 3. 701 ff.).

BELLONA.— F. Q. 3. 9. 22; 7. 6. 3; S. C. Oct. 114.

Bellona, the Roman goddess of war, is identified by Spenser with Pallas, the Greek goddess of armed resistance. This we know from a note by E. K. explaining *S. C.* Oct. 114. She is here called " queint Bellona," an epithet referring to her peculiar birth from the head of her father, Jupiter. In support of this story Lucian is cited; therefore, see his dialogue between Hephæstus and Zeus.

This identification is preserved further in *F. Q.* 3. 9. 22, where Bellona is represented as having engaged in the slaughter of the giants, and as having killed Enceladus with her own spear. Compare with this Apoll. 1. 6. 1, where Minerva is said, not to have killed Enceladus with her spear, but to have thrown the island of Sicily upon him in his flight. There is a further discrepancy in the statement that this occurred upon Hæmus, which had been heaped high by him. Spenser is evidently thinking of the contest which Typhon waged with Jupiter on Hæmus — a description of which, in Apoll. 1. 6. 1, 2, 3, 4, follows immediately upon the story of the war with the giants. In *F. Q.* 7. 6. 3, however, the character of Bellona is represented as quite different from that of Pallas, who does not delight in war for its own sake; while Bellona, like the Greek Enyo, revels in the spirit of battle, and arouses enthusiasm in armies. See *Æn.* 8. 703.

BELUS.— F. Q. 4. 11. 15. See Founders of Nations.

BERECYNTHIAN (Goddess).— R. R. 6. See Cybele.

BIBLIS.— F. Q. 3. 2. 41.

We have here a slight reference to the unnatural love of Biblis for her brother Caunus. The horrible story of her passion, its frustration, and her final metamorphosis into a fountain, is related in detail by Ovid (*Met.* 9. 454 ff.).

BISALTIS.— F. Q. 3. 11. 41.

Spenser, alluding to the sad aspect of Neptune, says : —

Ne ought but deare Bisaltis ay could make him glad.

Met. 6. 117 is the source of this statement : ". . . aries Bisaltida fallis."

BOREAS. — F. Q. 1. 2. 33; 5. 11. 58; S. C. Feb. 225; R. R. 16; 26.

Boreas was the personification of the north wind, and as such is often referred to by the ancients (see *Æn.* 3. 687). There are accounts of various exploits accomplished by him which are in keeping with his blustering character, but Spenser makes no reference to them. Modified by the epithets "bleak," "wrathful," "blustering," "fell," and "colde," Boreas is simply another name for the north wind.

BRONTES. — F. Q. 4. 5. 37; 4. 11. 13.

From the first reference we learn that Brontes was a giant who, in the Lipari Islands, was associated with Pyracmon in forging thunderbolts for the use of Zeus — a passage whose source is evidently *Æn.* 8. 416 ff., where these two giants and a third, Steropes, are described, under the less generic name of Cyclops, as working at the subterranean forges.

Brontes is mentioned also in the list of sea-gods (*F. Q.* 4. 11. 13), for which see **Sea-Gods**.

CADMUS.

This hero is mentioned but three times by Spenser, and each time in a different capacity: he appears as the builder of the acropolis at Thebes (*F. Q.* 2. 9. 45); as the father of Agave (*V. G.* 22); and as the ancestor of two hostile brothers (*V. G.* 52).

The whole story of the founding of Thebes, the Bœotian city, by Cadmus, the son of Agenor, is related by Ovid (*Met.* 3. 876 ff.). Bidden by his father to recover his sister Europa, who had been carried away by Zeus, or never to show himself in his home-country again, Cadmus sets out upon his quest. It proves to be a futile one; and, as an exile, he turns to the oracle at Delphi for directions as to his future course. He is told to follow a cow, which he would meet, and, wherever she should lie down, on that spot to found a city. He obeys directions, follows the heifer, and on the allotted spot, by the aid of armed men, who had sprung from the teeth of a hostile dragon, Cadmus founds the city of Thebes, the famous citadel of which is referred to by Spenser. The same story, in briefer form, is related by Apollodorus (3. 4. 1). The two hostile brothers who are referred to in *V. G.* 52 are Eteocles and Polyneices. That they were "borne of Cadmus blood" is evident from the following table:—

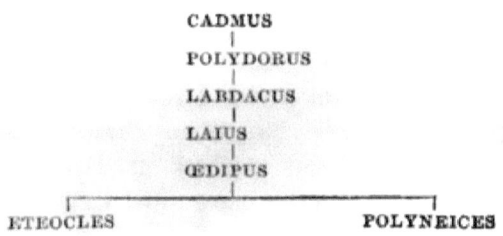

CAICUS.—F. Q. 4. 11. 14. See **Sea-Gods**.

CALLIOPE.—F. Q. 7. 6. 37; S. C. Apr. 100; S. C. June 57; T. M. 13. See **Muses**.

CAMILLA.—F. Q. 3. 4. 2.

This warrior maid, 'whom Diana contented, and who cherished an unchanging love for her darts and her virgin state,' is the most striking figure in *Æn.* 11. Surrounded by her select retinue of Italian virgins, she engages in fearless conflict with the Trojans and their allies; long is the list of those she slew, among whom was the Trojan Orsilochus.

CASSIOPEA.—F. Q. 1. 3. 16.

It is the chair of Cassiopea that is referred to here. The boastful pride of Cassiopea in her own beauty, and the vengeance of Neptune wreaked upon her daughter, have already been cited (see **Andromeda**). The further punishment of Cassiopea cannot better be described than by a translation of Hyginus, *Poet. Astron.* 2, Cassiopea: "Concerning her Euripides and Sophocles and many others have written, how she boasted that she surpassed the Nereids in beauty: for this her abode was fixed among the constellations, and she was seated upon a throne so that, as a punishment for her impiety, she seems, as the earth revolves, to move with her head bent backwards."

CELÆNO—F. Q. 2. 7. 23.

The picture which Spenser here paints of the harpy Celæno, sitting on a cliff, and singing a song so sad that it would melt a heart of stone, is a reproduction of *Æn.* 3. 245 ff. Æneas and his companions have landed on one of the Strophades. They kill some cattle and prepare a repast. No sooner are they seated to regale themselves than a band of harpies swoop down upon them and defile the viands. Virgil describes the harpies as foul monsters, having the faces of virgins, and the body, wings, and talons of sea-fowls. They are, moreover, always pale with consuming hunger. They have formerly inhabited Thrace, where they vexed the soothsayer Phineus (see Ap. Rh. 2. 178 ff.); but, driven thence by the Argonauts, they have since made the Strophades their haunt. After a combat with these monsters, Æneas and his men are forced to listen to a dire prophecy from the lips of Celæno, one of the harpies. She is described by Virgil as the prophetess of ill, seated upon a high rock, uttering the dire curse which shall follow the band of Trojans.

CERBERUS. — F. Q. 1. 5. 34; 1. 11. 41; 4. 10. 58; V. G. 44; 55.

The description of Cerberus in the first of these passages is patterned after Æn. 6. 417 ff. There, too, he is described as the monster that guarded the gates of hell, rearing his snakes in anger at the approach of Æneas. But in that case he is appeased by the Sibyl who accompanied Virgil, while Spenser says that it was Night who pacified the monster.

With the references to Cerberus in connection with the descent of Orpheus into hell, compare Georg. 4. 483; Met. 10. 11 ff.

CERES. — F. Q. 3. 1. 51, V. G. 26.

This Roman goddess of plenty is one with the Greek Demeter. Her character and attributes are vividly portrayed in the *Hymn to Ceres*, by Callimachus; and consistent with it are the numerous references to this goddess in later Greek and Latin writers, as well as the one from Spenser, which describes her as fruitful, and as bountifully pouring out her plenty. The *Hymn to Ceres* declares that to Triptolemus Ceres taught the art of agriculture.

CHARON. — V. G. 43.

For a description of Charon, the ferryman of the rivers in the Lower World, see Æn. 6. 298 ff.: "With his own hands he works the boat along with a pole, and manages the sails, and is always conveying to the shore the dead in his murky bark, old as he now is."

CHIMÆRA. — F. Q. 6. 1. 8 ; V. G. 8.

This monster is described by Homer (*Il.* 6. 179 ff.) as in front a lion, behind a dragon, in the middle a goat, and as breathing forth fire. He says further that she was killed by Bellerophon in Lycia, by the river Xanthus. Virgil (*Æn.* 6. 288) places this monster, with others, at the portals of the Lower World — a passage which no doubt furnished Spenser with his "fell Chimæra in her darksome den."

CHIRON. — F. Q. 7. 7. 40. See **Erigone**.

CHLORIS. — S. C. Apr. 122.

Chloris is here described as the chiefest nymph of all, and as wearing a crown of olives upon her head. E. K. (Spenser?), in his note on this passage, says : " *Cloris*, the name of a nymph and signifieth greenesse [χλωρός, *light green*], of whom is sayd, that Zephyrus, the westerne wind, being in love with her, and coveting her to wyfe, gave her for a dowrie the chiefdome and soveraigntye of al flowres, and green herbes, growing on earth." For this conception Spenser is plainly indebted to Ovid, *Fast.* 5. 195 ff., where Chloris is identified with Flora, and, as the wife of Zephyrus, has dominion over gardens and fields.

CHRYSAOR. — F. Q. 4. 11. 14. See **Sea-Gods**.

CICONES. — V. G. 68.

A people of Thrace who were auxiliaries of the Trojans. Attacked by Ulysses, after Troy was destroyed, they killed some of his men, and put the others to flight. Compare *Od.* 9. 38 ff.

CIMMERIANS. — T. M. 256 ; V. G. 47.

The dusky abode of the Cimmerians is a matter of dispute among the ancients : Homer (*Od.* 11. 14) places it in the Western world, — according to Strabo, near Lake Avernus in Italy, — and speaks of it as the entrance to the Lower World, whence Ulysses visited the shades. With this compare *V. G.* 47. Ovid, on the other hand (*Pont. Ep.* 4. 10), writing from Pontus, speaks of that country as the Cimmerian shore.

CLIMENE.—F. Q. 3. 11. 38. See Clymene.

CLIO.—F. Q. 3. 3. 4; 7. 6. 37. See Muses.

CLOTHO.—F. Q. 4. 2. 48; H. L. 63. See Fates.

CLYMENE.—F. Q. 3. 11. 38.

Spenser here alludes to her as the wife of Apollo and the mother of Phaeton. With this compare *Met.* 2. 19 ff.

COCYTUS.—F. Q. 1. 1. 37; 2. 7. 56; 3. 4. 55.

A river of the Lower World, mentioned in *Æn.* 6. 132, 297, 323. For *F. Q.* 1. 1. 37 see **Gorgon**.

CORONIS.—F. Q. 3. 11. 37.

We have here a reference to Coronis, the beloved of Apollo. Spenser says that, dying at the hands of Apollo, she was changed into a sweetbrier, and that afterwards Apollo tore his golden hair in remorse for his rash act.

Both Ovid (*Met.* 2. 542 ff.) and Hyginus (*Fab.* 202) relate this story of Apollo's jealousy regarding the unfaithfulness of his beloved Coronis. They both say that he killed her in anger, and Ovid adds that he repented of his cruelty when it was too late to restore her to life. There is, however, no authority for saying that she was turned into a sweetbrier; thus we have here another example of Spenser's original mythology.

CORYBANTES.—F. Q. 7. 6. 27. See Cybele.

CREUSA.—F. Q. 2. 12. 45. See Argonautic Expedition.

CUPID.

Spenser is not consistent in his treatment of the god of love, who appears so often in his poems: although, for the most part, he represents Cupid as the sportive boy of the later classics, yet in certain cases he deviates from this conception, and portrays the Cupid (Eros) of the early cosmogonies — that is, as one of the fundamental principles of nature, the power by which discordant elements were united and harmony brought out of chaos. Thus does Cupid figure in the lengthy passage on love in *Co. Cl.* (768 ff.), although even in this connection there are hints of the later Cupid in the references to his tyrannical spirit, his bow and arrows, etc. In the *Hymne of Love* also we meet the cosmogonic Cupid. This conception was, no doubt, suggested by a passage in Plato's *Symposium*; that, in turn, being founded upon *Theog.* 120 ff., where Eros is represented as a resistless power, born of Chaos. The story of Cupid's birth from Poros (Plenty) and Penia (Poverty) is also taken from the *Symposium*. Indeed, the *Hymne of Love* and the *Hymne of Beautie* are evidences of Plato's influence over Spenser.

The reference to Cupid's being awakened to life by Clotho may have been suggested by Orph. *Arg.* 15, where he is represented as the first of all the gods to emerge from Chaos. According to the several attributes of the Fates, it would be Clotho, rather than Lachesis or Atropos, who would call souls to life. (See **Fates**.)

Spenser is at variance with himself regarding the parentage of Cupid. In *Co. Cl.* 801 he represents him as born of Venus, but without a father, since Venus was of both sexes (a classical conception, for which see Serv. *Æn.* 2. 632). Compare also *F. Q.* 4. 10. 41. On the other hand, in *F. Q.* 1. Int. 3, Spenser declares Cupid to be the son of Jove and Venus. This would make Jove both the father and grandfather of Cupid, as in Virgil's *Ciris*, 134 — a passage to be explained in the light of Eurip. *Hip.* 534.

In other passages (*F. Q.* 2. 8. 6; 3. 6. 20; 4. Int. 5; 4. 12. 13; 6. 7. 37; *Mui.* 98; *H. L.* and *H. B. passim*; *Pro.* 96; *Epigrams* 1, 3, 4) Cupid is referred to as the son of Venus simply, without reference to his father. The *Symposium*, again, as well as numerous other passages from classical literature, might be quoted in support of these.

In *F. Q.* 3. 6. 50 Cupid and Psyche are represented as dwelling together in a state of bliss, and Pleasure is their child. See **Psyche**, and compare *Mui.* 126 ff.; *H. L.* 288.

As said above, Spenser's usual conception of Cupid corresponds to that of the later classics: he is "a faire, young, lusty boy" (*F. Q.* 7. 7. 46).

We read of his conquests over the gods — Jove, Phœbus, Neptune, Saturn, Bacchus, and Mars — in *F. Q.* 3. 11. 30 ff.; 2. 6. 35 (see the several headings); and of his resistless dominion over men (*F. Q.* 3. 1. 39; 3. 11. 46; 4. 9. 2; 6. 8. 25).

His power is spoken of as a snare (*F. Q.* 1. 10. 30); as a yoke (*Co. Cl.* 566); as a wanton rage (*F. Q.* 2. 9. 18), and the exhibition of it as wanton sports (*F. Q.* 2. 9. 34).

He is represented as blind (*Epigram* 1; *F. Q.* 6. 7. 32); as winged (*Am.* 60); as armed with bows and arrows (*F. Q.* 2. 9. 34; *Epigram* 2); in *Co. Cl.* 807 these shafts are described as of gold and lead. (See **Daphne**.)

In support of all these references, we cannot do better than quote from E. K.'s Glosse on *S. C.* March: "*Swaine*, a boye: for so he is described of the Poetes to be a boye, s. alwayes freshe and lustie: blindfolded, because he maketh no differences of personages: wyth divers colored winges, s. ful of flying fancies: with bowe and arrow, that is, with glaunce of beautye, which prycketh as a forked arrowe. He is sayd also to have shafts, some leaden, some golden: that is, both pleasure for the gracious and loved, and sorrow for the lover that is disdayned or forsaken. But who lists more at large to behold Cupids colours and furniture, let him reade ether Propertius, or Moschus, his Idyllion of *winged love*, being now most excellently translated into Latine by the singuler learned man, Angelus Politianus."

The scene in *F. Q.* 3. 6. 20 ff., where Venus is hunting for the runaway Cupid, was probably suggested by the poem of Moschus referred to above.

Of the four epigrams on Cupid, so in harmony with the later conception of him, the fourth will be recognized as an amplification of Theoc. *Idyl* 19; the second and third as translations of two epigrams by Clément Marot — *De Diane* and *De Cupido et de sa Dame*.

CYBELE. — F. Q. 1. 6. 15; 4. 11. 28; R. R. 6.

This is the name for a Phrygian divinity who became identified with the Greek Rhea. Spenser uses a strictly classical expression when he calls her "the mother of the gods" (*F. Q.* 4. 11. 28). Hesiod (*Theog.* 453 ff.) says that, as the wife of Saturn, she became the mother of Vesta, Ceres, Juno, Pluto, Neptune, and Jove; and the epithet, "mother of the gods," is frequently used by the ancients to designate this divinity. See, in particular, Ovid's description of the introduction of Cybele into Rome (*Fast.* 4. 249 ff.). Here she is called, again and again, "the mother," or "the mother of the gods."

Among her numerous other names was Berecynthia, or, as in *R. R.* 6, the Berecynthian goddess. Servius, commenting upon *Æn.* 6. 785, where this name is used, says: "Nam Berecynthos castellum est Phrygiæ juxta Sangarium fluvium, ubi mater deùm colitur." This passage, as a whole, doubtless suggested *R. R.* 6: the chariot, the crown of turrets, and the pride of Berecynthia in her mighty offspring, are the same. With these compare *F. Q.* 4. 11. 28, where there is the same classical conception. Servius comments thus upon *Æn.* 6. 786: "*turrita;* [*rel*] *quia ipsa est terra quae urbes sustinet.*" Ovid explains her turret crown from the fact that she gave towers to the earliest cities.

The frantic rites of Cybele are alluded to in *F. Q.* 1. 6. 15. Ovid (*Fast.* 4. 201 ff.) explains their origin by saying that when Rhea brought forth Jove in Crete, in order to conceal his cries from Saturn, who made a practice of devouring his children, the Curetes and the Corybantes beat shields and rattled empty helmets; and that the clash of the cymbals and other noises which attended the worship of the goddess in later times were survivals of the din on that occasion. Thus Homer sings in the *Hymn to the Mother of the Gods:* —

> Mother of all, both gods and men, commend,
> O Muse! whose fair form did from Jove descend;
> That doth with cymbal sounds delight her life,
> And tremulous divisions of the fife;
> Loves dreadful lions' roars, and wolves' hoarse howls,
> Sylvan retreats ; and hills, whose hollow knolls
> Raise repercussive sounds about her ears.

CYCONES. — V. G. 68. See Cicones.

CYMO. — F. Q. 4. 11. 51. See Nereids.

CYMOTHOE. — F. Q. 4. 11. 49. See Nereids.

CYNTHIA. — F. Q. 1. 1. 39; 1. 7. 34; 3. 1. 43. 7. 6. 8; 7. 6. 38; 7. 7. 50; S. C. Apr. 82; Aug. 89; Ep. 374; Pro. 121. See Diana.

CYPARISSUS. — F. Q. 1. 6. 17.

The details of the story of Cyparissus, as here cited, correspond to those of Ovid's version (*Met.* 10. 120 ff.), with this difference: while, with Spenser, it is Silvanus who loves the youth, according to Ovid it is Apollo. There is, however, the same disagreement among the ancients; thus Virgil implies that Cyparissus was beloved of Silvanus, when, in *Georg.* 1. 20, he represents the rustic god as bearing a cypress-tree, into which Ovid says that the youth was turned by Apollo.

DÆMOGORGON.—F. Q. 1. 5. 22; 4. 2. 47.

We cannot do better than quote the remarks of Dr. Jortin upon this point: "Gorgon: the same, I suppose, who is called Dæmogorgon by other modern writers, and by Spenser (*F. Q.* 1. 5. 22; 4. 2. 47).

"They give the name of Dæmogorgon to that terrible nameless divinity, of whom Lucan and Statius speak, when they introduce magicians threatening the infernal gods. Stat. *Theb.* 4. 514. Lucan, 6. 744.

"Dæmogorgon is a name which perhaps was unknown in the time of Lucan and Statius. However, it is to be found in Lactantius, The Scholiast of Statius, *Theb.* 4. 516. *Dicit deum Demogorgona summum.* It is also to be found in Hyginus, page 11. *Ex demogorgone et Terra, Python, draco divinus;* if the place be not corrupted."

DAMON.—F. Q. 4. 10. 27. See **Pythias.**

DANAE.—F. Q. 3. 11. 31.

We have here a brief account of Jove's intrigue with Danae. In this case he transformed himself into a shower of gold, and thus, deceiving the guard who had been placed to watch Danae, he won her. For the sources of this myth see *Met.* 6. 113 and Apoll. 2. 4. 1.

DAPHNE.—F. Q. 2. 12. 52; 3. 7. 26; 3. 11. 36; 4. 7. 22.

In the love of Apollo for Daphne we have another instance of the power of Cupid over the gods. In the first of these references, Spenser states that it was in the vale of Thessalian Tempe that "Fayre Daphne Phœbus hart with love did gore;" in the second her flight on the Ægean strand is referred to, as in the fourth also; in the third, we learn that Daphne did not return the love of Phœbus, and that the affair ended disastrously in her death.

An examination of the source of this myth (*Met.* 1. 452 ff.) reveals the fact that Cupid was the cause of all the trouble: Apollo had defied Cupid's power with the bow and arrow, and the wily god of love, to prove his might, lodged in the heart of Phœbus a golden, or love-exciting dart, and in the heart of Daphne, the daughter of the River Peneus in Thessaly, a leaden arrow, which would repel love. Thus did Daphne flee from the embrace of Apollo; and when all but overtaken, having prayed to her father Peneus for help, she was turned into a laurel. Apollo's loyalty to her memory is shown in his declaration: "My hair, my lyre, my quiver, shall always have thee, oh laurel."

DEMOPHOÖN.—V. G. 26.

The tree here referred to is the almond-tree (see Serv. *Ecl.* 5. 10) into which Phyllis was metamorphosed, when, grieving over the supposed fickleness of Demophoön, she had put an end to her life. Hyginus (*Fab.* 59) says that at a certain time the trees which sprang up at the death of Phyllis shed their leaves, thus mourning for her untimely end; hence the line: "Eternall hurte left unto many one."

DEUCALION.—F. Q. 3. 11. 42; 5. Int. 2.

The first of these passages states that Neptune turned himself into a dolphin to win the daughter of Deucalion. In recounting the intrigues of Neptune (*Met.* 6. 115 ff.), Ovid states that Melantho was thus won. For Spenser's authority in referring to Melantho as the daughter of Deucalion, see Tzet. *Lyc.* 208.

In the second passage, which refers to Deucalion and Pyrrha as casting stones behind their backs, Spenser follows *Met.* 1. 399 ff.

DIANA.

The sister of Apollo, whom the Greeks knew as Artemis, is designated by Spenser under the names of Cynthia, Diana, and Phœbe.

As Apollo was the god of the sun, she was the corresponding divinity of the moon. As Apollo was called Cynthius, on account of his birth at the foot of Mt. Cynthus, on the isle of Delos, so Diana was known as Cynthia for the same reason (compare *F. Q.* 7. 7. 50 with Hyg. *Fab.* 140); as he was Phœbus, she was known as Phœbe; and under these two names, Cynthia and Phœbe, Spenser often refers to her as the goddess of the moon.

In some instances he employs one of the names for the moon itself, as "When Phœbe shineth bright" (*S. C.* June 31; *Pro.* 121); but oftener he speaks of her "silver beams," "silver rays," "silver deaw," "silver face," or "silver bed." (See *F. Q.* 1. 1. 39; 1. 7. 34; 2. 1. 53; 2. 2. 44; 3. 1. 43; 4. 5. 14; 7. 6. 21; *S. C.* Apr. 65; Apr. 82; June 31; Aug. 89; Dec. 84; *Co. Cl.* 342; *Ep.* 149.)

Perhaps the most beautiful of the passages referring to the moon-goddess is that in which Mutability is described as climbing to the circle of the Moon (*F. Q.* 7. 6. 8 ff.).

Cynthia's place had been assigned to her by Jove, whose "dearest darling" Spenser elsewhere calls her (*F. Q.* 7. 7. 50). This is Spenser's only reference to the parentage of Cynthia. With this compare Hyg. *Fab.* 140.

There are numerous passages in the ancients which might be quoted to support this designation of Diana as the divinity of the moon; among them *Met.* 1. 11: "Nec nova crescendo reparabat corona Phœbe;" and *Æn.* 10. 216.

But Diana is not only the moon-goddess; she is also the goddess of the chase; and as such, armed with her bow and arrows (*F. Q.* 1. 6. 16), and surrounded by her nymphs in shady woods (*F. Q.* 1. 7. 5; 1. 12. 7; 3. 6. 16; 7. 6. 38), we frequently meet her upon the pages of Spenser. It is in this capacity, as "queen of archery," that she is celebrated in the *Hom. Hymn to Diana.* In the *Iliad* (21. 470) she is described as "the queen of wild beasts, huntress Artemis." Ovid (*Fast.* 2. 155) calls her "jaculatrix," and pictures her in the woods, resting from the chase, with her nymphs. Virgil (*Æn.* 1. 498 ff.) compares Dido, advancing to the temple, attended by her retinue of youths, to Diana, in these words: "As on the banks of Eurotas or over the ridges of Cynthus, Diana leads her dances, a thousand mountain-nymphs follow her and throng around; she wears her quiver on her shoulder, and as she steps along o'ertops all the goddesses; Latona's heart with silent joy rebounds." With this passage compare *F. Q.* 2. 3. 31.

As the friend of the huntsman Hippolytus, Diana appears in *F. Q.* 1. 5. 39 and 5. 8. 43. For this see **Hippolytus**.

As " queen of archery," delighting in the hardy sports of the chase, Diana scorns the gentler joys of love. Thus she is the champion of virginity in *F. Q.* 2. 2. 8, transforming a nymph into a stone to save her from the advances of Faunus. This incident was probably suggested by Diana's transformation of Arethusa to a fountain to save her from the love of Alpheus (*Met.* 5. 618 ff.), or by the metamorphosis of Daphne to a laurel (*Met.* 1. 548).

Thus, averse to love and under the vow of virginity, Diana is out of all harmony with Venus, the goddess of love, and her son, the sportive Cupid. The contrasting pleasures of the two are thus summed up by Spenser:—

> As you [Diana], in woods and wanton wildernesse
> Your glory sett to chace the salvage beasts,
> So my [Venus'] delight is all in joyfulnesse,
> In beds, in bowres, in banckets, and in feasts.
> *F. Q.* 3. 6. 22.

These words are spoken by Venus, who, in search of Cupid, has strayed into the woods of Diana, and surprised the virgin goddess in disarray — a situation evidently suggested by the story of Actæon (*Met.* 3. 131 ff.). "Whiles all her Nymphes did like a girlond her disclose," is but a paraphrase of "circumfusæque Dianam Coporibus texere suis" (line 180). This same intrusion of Actæon furnished the basis for the myth concerning Faunus, which Spenser constructs in *F. Q.* 7. 6. 37 ff. That he had this in mind is shown by the lines:—

> And eft him placed where he close might view
> That never any saw, save onely one,
> Who, for his hire to so foole-hardy dew,
> Was of his hounds devour'd in Hunter's hew.

In *Epigram* 2, Diana, in the course of her chase, comes upon Cupid asleep, and exchanges arms with him. See **Cupid**.

But even Cynthia became a victim of the archer-god. The

story of Endymion, the Latmian shepherd, which has ever been a favorite with the poets, is referred to in *S. C.* July 63 and *Ep.* 374. With these passages compare Theocritus, *Idyl* 20.

In *Ep.* 374 Spenser says that the Latmian shepherd won the affections of Cynthia by presenting her with "a fleece of wool." But Virgil (*Georg.* 3. 391) says that it was Pan who did this.

For Diana's part in the death of Orion (*F. Q.* 7. 7. 39), see **Orion.**

DICE. — F. Q. 5. 9. 32. See **Litæ.**

DODONIAN (Tree). — V. B. 5. 1. See **Jove.**

DOLON. — V. G. 67. 8.

"Dolon's subtile surprysall" is explained by *Il.* 10. 314 ff. Setting out from the Trojan camp as a spy, he was waylaid by Ulysses and Diomedes, and killed.

DORIS. — F. Q. 4. 11. 48.

Among those who came to the wedding of the Medway and the Thames was "the gray-eyde Doris," the daughter of Ocean, the wife of Nereus, and the mother of the fifty Nereids, who attended her. For Spenser's authority on this point see *Theog.* 240 ff.

DORIS. — F. Q. 4. 11. 49. See **Nereids.**

DOTO. — F. Q. 4. 11. 48. See **Nereids.**

DRYOPE. — F. Q. 1. 6. 15.

This nymph, here mentioned as the wife of Silvanus, is evidently the same as the one of *Æn.* 10. 551, who is said to be the wife of Faunus. This discrepancy is to be accounted for by the similarity between the rustic divinities, Silvanus and Faunus — a similarity which often led to their identification by the classical authors.

DYNAMENE. — F. Q. 4. 11. 49. See **Nereids.**

ECHIDNA. — F. Q. 5. 10. 10; 5. 11. 23; 6. 6. 10 ff.

The last of these references begins thus : —

> Echidna is a Monster direfull dred,
> Whom Gods doe hate, and heavens abhor to see.

She is further described as of hideous shape and huge head, — a combination of maiden and dragon. On account of her dreadful aspect, she is condemned by the gods to live in obscurity with the blustering Typhaon, among rocks and caves. By him she is the mother of a hellish dog, "that hight the Blatant Beast."

These details correspond closely to those given by Hesiod (*Theog.* 295 ff.). He says that Echidna and Typhaon were the parents of various monsters, among them Orthrus, the dog of Geryon. This, of course, served as a suggestion to our poet for making them the parents of the Blatant Beast. Elsewhere (*F. Q.* 5. 10. 10) Spenser says that Echidna and Typhaon were the parents of Orthrus.

EIONE. — F. Q. 4. 11. 50. See **Nereids**.

EIRENE. — F. Q. 5. 9. 32. See **Litæ**.

ELYSIAN FIELDS. — F. Q. 4. 10. 23; S. C. Nov. 179; B. T. 332; V. G. 53.

E. K. says in the Glosse on *S. C.* Nov. 179: "*Elysian fields*, be devised of Poetes to be a place of pleasure like Paradise, where the happy soules doe rest in peace and eternal happynesse." In the other passages also the Elysian Fields are referred to as the "abode of the blessed." Compare with these *Æn.* 6. 638 ff., 747, where the Elysian Fields are described as regions of joy, possessed by the happy few.

ENCELADUS. — F. Q. 3. 9. 22. See **Bellona**.

ENDORE. — F. Q. 4. 11. 48. See **Nereids**.

EPHIALTES. — V. G. 47.

Otus, who is here mentioned in close connection, and Ephialtes, were known as the Aloidæ, and were giants of huge bulk.

In their presumption they dared attempt to invade heaven itself by piling Ossa on Olympus, and Pelion upon Ossa; but before they accomplished their end, Apollo killed them with his shafts. Thus Homer relates their death (*Od.* 11. 305 ff.), though Apollodorus and others account for it in another way. Hyginus (*Fab.* 28) adds that afterwards, in the Lower World, these giant brothers, placed back to back, were bound with serpents to a column, — a slightly different situation from that described in the passage under consideration.

A corrupt text of *V. G.* would account for the unauthorized statement that these brothers attempted to burn the world: some texts here read " incendere " instead of " rescindere," which is more in keeping with classical tradition.

ERATO.—F. Q. 4. 11. 49. See Nereids.

EREBUS.

     ÆTERNITIE
      |
     HEREBUS (M. NIGHT)
      |
     PHLEGETHON
      F. Q. 2. 4. 41; 3. 4. 55.

Eternity seems to be the same as the Chaos of Hesiod (*Theog.* 123), whence all things proceeded. Among the offspring of Chaos, Hesiod mentions Erebus and his sister Night — Erebus being a personification of darkness. Spenser further follows Hesiod in making Erebus the husband of Night. While Hesiod calls only the Sky and Day the children of this union, later writers — such as Hyginus, in the preface to his fables — multiply their offspring, among whom Styx is mentioned. Thus Spenser is following the spirit, if not the letter, of classical mythology in calling Erebus and Night the parents of Phlegethon, another river of the Lower World.

In *F. Q.* 3. 4. 55 and *V. G.* 40, Erebus is used without personification, also, as the abode of Night, the region of darkness. Compare *Æn.* 6. 247, 404 and *Met.* 10. 76, where it signifies the Infernal Regions.

ERICHTHONIAN (tower).—V. G. 71.

This is Pergamum, the Trojan citadel, put by synecdoche for Troy itself. Erichthonius, for whom it is called, was a son of Dardanus, the ancestor of the Trojans. After the death of his brother Ilus, he ruled the kingdom. (See Apoll. 3. 12. 2.)

ERIGONE.—F. Q. 3. 11. 43.

Spenser says that for love of Erigone, Saturn transformed himself to a centaur; and, in the same connection, that Liber (Bacchus) won Philyra in the form of a fruitful vine. By comparison with *Met.* 6. 125, 126, we find that Spenser has turned the names around, and that it was Liber who won Erigone, while Saturn deceived her who became by him the mother of the two-formed Chiron. Though Ovid does not give her name, we know from Apoll. 1. 2. 4 and Ap. Rh. 2. 1241 that it was Philyra.

It is to be noticed in this connection that in *F. Q.* 7. 7. 40 (which forms a part of the description of the procession of months), November is represented as riding upon "a dreadfull centaure . . . the seed of Saturn and of faire Nais, Chiron hight." This seeming discrepancy is explained by the fact that Spenser here employs Nais (a Greek generic noun, meaning *water-nymph*) as a proper name to denote Philyra, a usage which may have been suggested by Ap. Rh. 4. 813, where Philyra is referred to as a Naiad. See also Schol. Ap. Rh. 813.

ERINNYS.— F. Q. 2. 2. 29; V. G. 50.

The adjective "fell" is well applied to Erinnys, originally the personification of persecuting anger. A plurality of such personifications were known as the Erinnyes, Eumenides, Furiæ, or Diræ. With earlier writers their number is not limited, but later writers say they are three in number (*Æn.* 12. 845 ff.).

In the passage before us, Spenser represents Erinnys as the personification of discord rather than as an unrelenting curse, the classical conception (*Il.* 9. 571; *Met.* 1. 241).

ERYX.— F. Q. 4. 11. 14. See Sea-Gods.

EUAGORE.— F. Q. 4. 11. 50. See Nereids.

EUARNA.— F. Q. 4. 11. 51. See Nereids.

EUCRATE.— F. Q. 4. 11. 48. See Nereids.

EULIMENE.— F. Q. 4. 11. 49. See Nereids.

EUNICA.— F. Q. 4. 11. 49. See Nereids.

EUNOMIA.— F. Q. 5. 9. 32. See Litæ.

EUPHEMUS.— F. Q. 4. 11. 14. See Sea-Gods.

EUPHROSYNE.— F. Q. 6. 10. 22. See Graces.

EUPOMPE.— F. Q. 4. 11. 51. See Nereids.

EUROPA.—F. Q. 3. 11. 30; 5. Int. 5; 7. 7. 33; Mui. 278.

With the references to the seduction of Europa by Jove, in the form of a bull, compare *Met.* 6. 103; 2. 833; Moschus, *Europa*; Apoll. 3. 1. 1. For the presence of this bull among the constellations (5. Int. 5), see Hyg. *Poet. Astron.* 2. Taurus.

EURYDICE.—R. T. 391; V. G. 55; 58.

These passages pertain to the disappearance of Eurydice and her futile rescue by Orpheus, for which see **Orpheus**.

Daph. 463 ff., reads:—

> But, as the mother of the Gods, that sought
> For faire Eurydice, her daughter deere,
> Throughout the world, with wofull heavy thought;

The classics furnish no authority for making Eurydice the daughter of the mother of the Gods; nor for the statement that Eurydice, upon her disappearance, was sought far and wide by her mother. Thus we have here another deviation from classical mythology: our poet seems to have had in mind the story of Ceres and Proserpina. Since, however, Cybele, who was usually called the mother of the gods, and Ceres (Demeter) were often identified by the ancients, Spenser simply errs in the name of the daughter, putting Eurydice for Proserpina. See also *S. C.* Oct. 29.

EURYNOME.—F. Q. 6. 10. 22. See Graces.

EURYPULUS.—F. Q. 4. 11. 14. See Sea-Gods.

EURYTION.—F. Q. 5. 10. 10.

From this passage we learn that Eurytion was the cowherd of the giant Geryon—a statement confirmed by Apoll. 2. 5. 10. See **Geryon**.

EURYTUS.—F. Q. 4. 11. 14. See Sea-Gods.

FATES.

Spenser says that the dwelling of the Fates is in Chaos (*F. Q.* 4. 2. 47). He names three sisters,—Clotho, Lachesis, and Atropos,—and represents the first as holding the distaff, the second as spinning out the thread, and the third as cutting it in two.

For his conception of the abode of the Fates, our poet is indebted to the classical idea of their parentage. According to Hesiod (*Theog.* 217), they are the daughters of Night, whose parent was Chaos; or, according to Cic. *De Nat. Deor.* 3. 44, of Erebus and Night.

In regard to the picture which Spenser draws of the Fates, intent upon their all-important work — one familiar to us in art as well as literature — we cannot do better than quote from E. K.: " *The fatall sisters*, Clotho, Lachesis, and Atropos, daughters of Herebus and the Nighte, whom the Poetes fayne to spinne the life of man, as it were a long threde, which they drawe out in length, till his fatal houre and timely death be come; but if by other casualtie his dayes be abridged, then one of them, that is, Atropos, is sayde to have cut the threde in twain. Hereof commeth a common verse, ' Clotho colum bajulat, Lachesis trahit, Atropos occat.' " — Note on *S. C.* Nov. 148. The quotation with which this note closes is in *Anth. Lat.* 792.

For the boasted superiority of the Fates over gods and men (*F. Q.* 4. 2. 51), see **Jove**.

The awakening of Cupid from Chaos (*H. L.* 63) is said to be at the hands of Clotho. See **Cupid**.

FAUNUS.— F. Q. 2. 2. 7; 7. 6. 42.

For the sources of both these references see **Diana**.

FLORA.— F. Q. 1. 1. 48; 1. 4. 17; 2. 12. 50; S. C. March 16; May 31.

" *Flora*, the Goddesse of flowres, but indede (as saith Tacitus) a famous harlot, which, with the abuse of her body having gotten great riches, made the people of Rome her heyre : who, in remembraunce of so great beneficence, appointed a yearley feste for the memoriall of her, calling her, not as she was, or as some doe think, Andronica, but **Flora**; making her the Goddesse of floures, and doing yerely to her solemne sacrifice." — Note by E. K. on *S. C.* March 16. See also **Chloris**.

FOUNDERS OF NATIONS. — F. Q. 4. 11. 15. ff.

Following upon the list of Sea-Gods is a list of others who were also sons of Neptune, but with the distinction that they were also the founders of powerful nations: —

Ogyges. — "Ancient Ogyges, even th' auncientest." According to Tzet. *Lyc.* 1206, he was a son of Poseidon. He was the first ruler of Thebes, and Bœotia was called, after him, Ogygia (Strab. 9. 2. 18). Spenser appropriately lays the stress upon his great age, since the Greek adjective ὠγύγιος means "primeval."

Inachus "renowmd above the rest." According to Apoll. 2. 1. 1 he was a river-god and son of Oceanus. He was the founder of Argos. See **Inachus**.

Phœnix. — A son of Agenor, — and therefore grandson of Neptune. He founded Phœnicia. (Apoll. 3. 1. 1.)

Aon. — A son of Neptune, from whom Bœotia derived its name Aonia. See Stat. *Theb.* 1. 34; Paus. 9. 5. 1.

Pelasgus "old." Apollodorus (2. 1. 1) says that, according to Acusilaus, Pelasgus was identical with Argus, who was a descendant of Ocean and Tethys, and that from him the name Pelasgia was given to the Peloponnesus; and others mention him as the ancestor of the Pelasgians, the earliest inhabitants of Greece.

Belus "great." According to Diod. Sic. 1. 28. 1, he was a son of Neptune and founder of Babylon.

Phœax (Phæax), a son of Neptune and progenitor of the Phæacians, the early inhabitants of Corcyra. (Diod. Sic. 4. 72. 3.)

Agenor "best," son of Neptune and founder of a kingdom (Sidon) in Phœnicia. (Apoll. 2. 1. 4.) There seems to be no particular reason for calling him "best."

Albion.

> And mightie Albion, father of the bold
> And warlike people which the Britaine Islands hold.

Spenser is indebted to Holinshed's *History of England* (1. 3) for this story. See **Hercules**.

GALATEA.—F. Q. 4. 11. 49. See **Nereids.**

GALENE.—F. Q. 4. 11. 48. See **Nereids.**

GERYON.—F. Q. 5. 10. 9.

Spenser describes Geryon as a giant, with "three bodies powre in one combynd," who ruled Spain with great oppression. He further speaks of his purple kine, his cowherd Eurytion, and Orthrus, the dog that watched these cattle, and closes with the statement that all were overcome by Hercules. See **Hercules.**

In saying that Geryon fed these oxen with the flesh of human beings, Spenser follows Natalis Comes rather than any classical authority.

GLAUCE.—F. Q. 4. 11. 48. See **Nereids.**

GLAUCONOME.—F. Q. 4. 11. 50. See **Nereids.**

GLAUCUS.—F. Q. 4. 11. 13. See **Sea-Gods.**

GORGON.—F. Q. 1. 1. 37. See **Dæmogorgon.**

GORGONIAN (shield).—F. Q. 3. 9. 22. See **Ægide** (shield).

GRACES.—F. Q. 6. 10. 21.

The ancients by no means agree as to the number, names, and parentage of the Graces. In order to show this, we cannot do better than quote from the *Greece* of Pausanias (9. 35). He says: "The Bœotians, too, say that Eteocles was the first that sacrificed to the Graces. And, indeed, that he established three Graces they are well convinced, but they have lost the remembrance of the names which he gave them. For the Lacedæmonians only worship two Graces, the statues of which, they say, were dedicated by Lacedæmon, the son of Taygete, who also gave them the names of Cleta and Phaenna. These names, indeed, are very properly given to the Graces, as likewise are those names which are assigned to the Graces by the Athenians, for the Athenians have from ancient times venerated the Graces, Auxo and Hegemone. Indeed we now pray to three Graces, having learnt there are three from the Orchomenian Eteocles. And at Athens, in the vestibule of the tower, there are three Graces whose mysteries, which are kept secret from the multitude, are celebrated.

"But Pamphus is the first we are acquainted with that celebrated the Graces in verse; but he neither mentions their number nor their names. Homer, too, makes mention of the Graces, and says that one of these is the wife of Vulcan, and that her name is Charis. He also says that Sleep is the lover of the Grace Pasithea, and in the speech of Sleep he has the following verse: —

> That she my loved one shall be ever mine,
> The youngest Grace, Pasithea the divine.

Hence some have suspected that Homer knew of other more ancient Graces.

"But Hesiod in his *Theogony* says that the Graces are the daughters of Jupiter and Eurynome, and that their names are Aglaia, Thalia, and Euphrosyne.

"But Antimachus neither mentions the number nor the names of the Graces, but only says they are the daughters of Aigle and the Sun."

In the passage under consideration, then, we see that Spenser follows Hesiod (*Theog.* 907 ff.) in the number, name, and parentage of the Graces. In *T. M.* 403, however, he says that they are the offspring of Venus: this is but a slight exaggeration of the conception which made the Graces the special attendants of Venus, as in this passage, and *F. Q.* 6. 10. 9; 6. 10. 15; 6. 10. 21; *Ep.* 108. Very numerous are the passages in the classics that might be quoted as pictures of Venus attended by the Graces: in the *Hom. Hymn to Venus*,

> The ready Graces wait, her baths prepare,
> And oint with fragrant oils her flowing hair.

See also *Od.* 8. 364; Hor. *Carm.* 1. 4; 1. 30; 3. 21; 4. 7.

The exposition which Spenser gives of the function of the Graces and the description and explanation of the usual representations of these sisters find appropriate comment in a note by E. K. on *S. C.* Apr. 109: —

"The Graces be three sisters, the daughters of Jupiter, (whose names are Aglaia, Thalia, Euphrosyne; and Homer oneley added a fourth, s. Pasithea) otherwise called Charites, that is, thankes: whom the Poetes feyned to be the Goddesses of all bountie and comelines, which therefore (as sayth Theodontius) they make three, to wete, that men first ought to be gracious and bountifull to other freely; then to receive benefits at other mens hands courteously; and thirdly, to requite them thankfully; which are three sundry Actions in liberalitye. And Boccace saith, that they be painted naked (as they were indeed on the tombe of C. Julius Cæsar) the one having her back toward us, and her face fromwarde, as proceeding from us; the other two toward us, noting double thanke to be due to us for the benefit we have done." See also Seneca, *De Benef.* 1. 3, for a lengthy discussion upon the Graces.

The indefinite number of Graces, of which the poet writes in 6. 10. 21, is also corroborated by classical authority. Thus E. K. says:—

"Many Graces, though there be indeede but three Graces or Charites (as afore is sayd) or at the utmost but foure, yet, in respect of many gyftes of bounty there may be sayde more. And so Musæus sayth, that in Heroes eyther eye there sat a hundred Graces. And, by that authoritye, thys same Poete, in his *Pageaunts*, saith 'An hundred Graces on her eyelidde sate,' etc."— Note on *S. C.* June 25.

HEBE.— R. T. 384; H. L. 283; Ep. 405.

The first two of these passages refer to Hebe as the wife of Hercules, after the apotheosis of the latter. In other words, after the earthly life of labor which Hercules led, he is borne to Heaven, and, in recognition of his glorious deeds, eternal youth (for Hebe is the personification of youth) is conferred upon him. See *Theog.* 950 ff.; *Od.* 11. 603; Apoll. 2. 7. 7; *Hom. Hymn to Hercules.*

In *Ep.* 405, Hebe is invoked for offspring along with Hymen.

HECATE.— F. Q. 1. 1. 43; 7. 6. 3.

In the latter passage Hecate is mentioned as one of the Titans (see **Titans**), who by special favor of Jove, after the fall of the Titans, retained all rule and principality. For her extensive power over gods and men, to which Spenser here alludes, see the lengthy tribute paid to Hecate by Hesiod (*Theog.* 411 ff.). But we must look elsewhere for the source of the first reference, where the name of Hecate is called "dreaded," implying that she was an infernal divinity; for while Hesiod and other earlier writers attribute to her all power over heaven, earth, and sea, they do not mention her in connection with the Lower World. We must turn to later writers for this conception. Thus Virgil (*Æn.* 6. 247) declares that the power of Hecate extends over both heaven and hell. She was regarded as a being of grewsome aspect, practiced in sorcery and witchcraft. Thus it will be remembered that it was to Hecate that Medea owed her skill in magic charms (see Ap. Rh. 3. *passim*).

HECTOR.—F. Q. 2. 9. 45; V. G. 63; 65; 66; R. R. 14.

The first of the passages refers to the fate of Astyanax, the child of Hector. After the capture of Troy he was hurled from the tower of Ilium by the Greeks. See *Met.* 13. 415 ff.; Hyg. *Fab.* 109. For the other references, see **Achilles** and **Æacides**.

HELEN.

As the prize bestowed upon Paris for his judgment in regard to the beauty of Venus, and as the consequent cause of the Trojan War, Helen is referred to in *F. Q.* 2. 7. 55; 3. 9. 35; 4. 11. 19. See **Venus** and **Nereus**.

The last of these passages refers to her as the Tindarid lass — that is, the daughter of Tyndareus. Compare *Æn.* 2. 601; *Met.* 15. 23.

In *F. Q.* 3. 10. 12 Spenser represents Helen as overjoyed at the sight of Troy in flames. This seems to have been suggested by the story of Deiphobus in regard to the conduct of Helen on the night that the Greeks entered Troy (*Æn.* 6. 517): "She, in feigned religious dance, led around the city the Phrygian women, raising the bacchanal cry; she herself in their midst held a mighty firebrand, and called in the Greeks from the height of the citadel."

The incident referred to in *Co. Cl.* 920 is related of the poet Stesichorus: he was said to have written an attack upon Helen, and in consequence to have been struck with blindness, only recovering his sight after he had atoned for his fault by a recantation, beginning: "False is that word of mine." See Plat. *Phæd.*

HELLE. — F. Q. 3. 11. 30; 5. Int. 5.

The familiar myth which represents Phrixus and Helle escaping upon a "golden fleecy ram" from the cruelty of their step-mother, Ino, is touched upon in both these passages, the first of which declares that this ram was Jove in disguise, who thus deceived Helle. This seems at first an unwarranted perversion of the usual myth, which states that the ram, the offspring of Neptune and Theophane, was brought to Phrixus and Helle by their own mother Nephele, in order that they might escape from the snares of Ino (see Hyg. *Fab.* 3; 188; Apoll. 1. 9. 1); but there is a slight authority for it in Ovid, *Fast.* 4. 715.

HERCULES.

The parentage of this hero is referred to in *R. T.* 380 and *Ep.* 328. He was the son of Jove and Alcmena. (See **Alcmena.**) Spenser calls him not only *Hercules*, but also *Alcides*, the *Amphytrionide*, the *Œtean Knight*, and the *Tirynthian groome*. The two patronymics are explained by the following table: —

      PERSEUS
        |
      ALCÆUS
        |
      AMPHITRYON (STEPFATHER OF HERCULES)
        |
      HERCULES

The epithet, *Tirynthian groome*, is accounted for by the fact that Hercules was brought up at Tiryns, in Argolis, and was, therefore, often called the *Tirynthian hero* by the ancient writers. Thus Servius explains *Æn.* 7. 662. See also Call. *Hymn to Diana*, 146; Paus. 10. 13. 8.

Hercules is appropriately alluded to as the Œtean Knight, because it was from Mt. Œta that he was carried to heaven.

Of the twelve great labors which Hercules accomplished for Eurystheus, and by which he won immortality, Spenser mentions six. They are as follows: —

The **Nemean Lion.** — F. Q. 2. 5. 31; 7. 7. 36; Mui. 70 ff.

The **Lernean Hydra.** — F. Q. 1. 7. 17; 6. 12. 32; R. R. 10; V. B. 10.

The **Mares of Diomedes.** — F. Q. 5. 8. 31.

The **Oxen of Geryon.** — F. Q. 5. 10. 10.

The Golden Apples of the Hesperides. — F. Q. 2. 7. 54; Am. 77.

Cerberus. — F. Q. 6. 12. 35.

It is probable that Spenser drew these references from Apoll. 2 or from Diod. Sic. 4, both of whom relate in detail all the twelve labors of Hercules.

Besides the so-called twelve labors of Hercules, the ancients recount subordinate adventures also. Such, for instance, is the fight with the Centaurs, mentioned by Spenser in *F. Q.* 4. 1. 23. While in quest of the Erymanthian boar, Hercules came to the cave of the Centaur Pholus. There, in spite of the protests of Pholus, he opened a jar of wine, and the neighboring Centaurs, attracted by the odor, rushed into the cave; whereupon the fight alluded to took place. In support of this see Apoll. and Diod. Sic., whose accounts of this affair agree in the main.

A review of the labors of Hercules reveals the fact that they were not confined to the East. Thus the conquest of Geryon took place in the island Eurythea, off the coast of Spain; and while on this expedition Hercules erected the pillars referred to in *Pro.* 148. (See Apoll. and Diod. Sic.)

The exploits of Hercules in the West, which are related by Apollodorus and Diodorus Siculus, are summed up by Spenser thus : —

> Who all the West with equall conquest wonne,
> And monstrous tyrants with his club subdewed.
>
> *F. Q.* 5. 1. 2.

Spenser mentions further the contest between Albion of Britain and the Celtic Hercules of France — perhaps a native hero who was identified with the Greek Hercules (*F. Q.* 2. 10. 11; 4. 11. 16). While Spenser, no doubt, took this particular incident from the British Chroniclers, Diodorus Siculus gives ample testimony to the founding of the Gallic nation by Hercules (5. 24. 2 ff.).

But even so mighty a conqueror as Hercules was himself subdued by the darts of Cupid. *F. Q.* 5. 5. 24 represents him as in the society of Iole, forgetting war and delighting "In combats of sweet love," his huge club and rough lion's skin exchanged for a distaff and cloak of gold. See also *F. Q.* 5. 8. 2.

This picture is based upon classical authority, — probably

Ovid, *Her.* 9, — but Spenser makes a mistake, not in implying the love of Hercules for Iole (see Apoll. 2. 7. 7 ; *Met.* 9. 140), but in saying that it was for her sake that he led an effeminate life. Our poet is evidently thinking of Omphale, queen of Lydia, with whom Hercules at one time passed several years. In the epistle by Ovid, cited above, Hercules' amour with Iole is mentioned by Deianira in close connection with her reproaches against her husband for his effeminate life with Omphale — a circumstance which may account for the confusion on the part of Spenser. For the affection of Hercules for Hylas (*F. Q.* 3. 12. 7 ; 4. 10. 27), see Hylas.

For his apotheosis and union with Hebe (*H. L.* 283), see Hebe.

> And on the other syde a pleasaunt grove
> Was shott up high, full of the stately tree
> That dedicated is t'Olympick Jove,
> And [of the tree which was dedicated] to his sonne
>   Alcides, whenas hee
> In Nemus gayned goodly victoree.
>
> *F. Q.* 2. 5. 31.

The above interpolation is necessary to a proper understanding of this passage; for the oak was sacred only to Jove, while it was the poplar which was dedicated to Hercules. See Virgil, *Ecl.* 7. 61. Spenser makes the triumph over the Nemean lion the immediate cause of this honor to Hercules — an idea which, so far as is known, is original with him.

Such are some of the points in the arduous life of Hercules. Well might Calliope, the muse who records the heroic, exclaim that she raised Hercules to heaven! (*T. M.* 461.)

HEREBUS. — F. Q. 2. 4. 41; 3. 4. 55; V. G. 40. See **Erebus**.

HERMES. — F. Q. 7. 6. 19 ff. See **Mercury**.

HESIONE. — V. G. 62.

As a parallel to this free translation of a much disputed passage in the original may be cited Apoll. 2. 6. 4 ; 3. 12. 7 and *Met.* 11. 194 ff., whence it appears that Hesione was given captive to Telamon by Hercules in reward for his valor when the latter attacked Troy, and that she afterwards became his wife.

HESPERUS. — F. Q. 1. 2. 6; 1. 7. 30; 3. 4. 51; Ep. 95; Pro. 164.

The ancients, even in the earliest times, regarded Hesperus, the evening-star, as identical with the morning-star; and thus Spenser is quite classical in employing the same name to denote respectively the evening-star (*F. Q.* 3. 4. 51) and the morning-star (*F. Q.* 1. 2. 6).

Both the Greeks and the Romans, however, referred to the morning-star as the bringer of light, calling it Ἑωσφόρος and Lucifer; and Spenser follows them when he describes Hesperus as "bringing forth dawning light." On this point see *Il.* 23. 226; and thus, also, Ovid assigns to Hesperus a dusky steed and to Lucifer a white one. (Compare *Fast.* 2. 314; 5. 419 with *Fast.* 15. 189; *Met.* 2. 115.) See also Hyg. *Poet. Astron.* 2. De quinque stellis.

The brilliancy of Hesperus, alluded to by Spenser, is described by Homer (*Il.* 22. 317) as a brightness surpassing that of the other stars of heaven.

In *F. Q.* 7. 6. 9 and *V. G.* 40, Vesper, the Latin word for "evening," is used for Hesperus, the evening star. Compare with such usage *Met.* 1. 63 and Horace, *Carm.* 2. 9.

HIPPOLYTUS. F. Q. 1. 5. 36 ff.

For convenience in tracing this myth to its sources, the following points made by Spenser may be enumerated: —

1. Hippolytus, a huntsman — son of Theseus.
2. Sought by his stepmother, whom he repels, in consequence of which she complains of him to Theseus.
3. Neptune, besought by Theseus, sends two sea-monsters, which so frighten the horses of Hippolytus, as he is driving, that he is killed. See also *F. Q.* 5. 8. 43.
4. The stepmother [Phædra], repenting, kills herself with a knife.
5. Theseus, upon learning the innocence of his son, rends his hair and tongue.
6. With the aid of Diana, who is the friend of Hippolytus, Theseus gathers up the remains of his son, and bears them to Æsculapius.
7. Æsculapius restores Hippolytus, and, in consequence, in-

curs the anger of Jove, who thrusts him down to hell with a thunderbolt.

A comparison of the above with *Æneid* 7. 765 ff., reveals the fact that Virgil makes or hints at the following points: 2; 3 (but no mention of the number of sea-monsters — simply in the plural); 6 (but nothing is said of Theseus' gathering the remains); 7.

Ovid (*Met.* 15. 497 ff.) touches upon 1 (but does not say Hippolytus was a huntsman); 2; 3 (but speaks of one monster only); 6 (but does not say that Theseus gathered his bones); 7 (nothing, however, of Jove's anger toward Æsculapius).

Ovid (*Fast.* 6. 737 ff.) mentions 1 (but does not speak of Hippolytus as a huntsman); 2; 3 (but only one monster, and nothing of the appeal of Theseus to Neptune); 6 (but does not say that Theseus gathered the remains of Hippolytus); 7.

It is evident from these comparisons that Spenser must have been indebted to some other source, or his own inventive powers, for the facts that Hippolytus was a huntsman, that Phædra stabbed herself, that Theseus tore his hair and tongue, and that he afterwards gathered together the remains of Hippolytus, and bore them to Æsculapius.

Turning to the drama of *Hippolytus* by Euripides, we find that the youth is a son of Theseus, and a huntsman, and specially devoted to Diana: —

> Artemis, Phœbos' sister, child of Zeus,
> He honors, thinking her the chief of gods;
> And ever in the greenwood with the maid
> Destroys the beasts with his fleet-footed hounds,
> Enjoying more than human comradeship.

Furthermore, points 2, 3, and 4 are clearly brought out, except that only one monster is mentioned, and that Phædra hangs herself, instead of committing suicide with a knife. Theseus learns of his son's innocence through Diana, but his grief finds vent in only controlled expressions of passion. Nothing is said of the revival of Hippolytus, who dies in the presence of his father.

One other source remains to be considered — the *Hippolytus* of Seneca. Here are brought out points 1, 2, 3 (but one monster only), and 4. Furthermore, Theseus learns of the innocence of Hippolytus through Phædra, whereupon he gives expression to his feelings in long speeches — not, however, in the way Spenser mentions. But, as in Euripides, nothing is said of the bones' being gathered up by Theseus, or of the revival of Hippolytus by Æsculapius.

It would appear from this discussion, then, that while Spenser follows Seneca in certain striking particulars, he is, for the rest of his story, indebted to the narratives of either Virgil or Ovid, and to his own fertile imagination.

HIPPOTHOE. — F. Q. 4. 11. 50. See Nereids.

HOURS. — F. Q. 7. 7. 45; Ep. 99.

These two passages really agree in regard to the parentage of the Hours, since the Jove of the one and the Day of the other are identical. The domain of Zeus being "the wide heaven, in clear air and clouds" (*Il.* 15. 192), he was sometimes identified by the ancients, as by Spenser, with the Upper World and the light, as contrasted with the Lower World, the darkness. See **Jove**.

In making Day and Night the parents of the Hours, Spenser is original. Hesiod (*Theog.* 901) calls them the daughters of Jove and Themis, — Eunomie, Dice, and Irene, — while Homer does not mention their parentage or names. It is, however, *Il.* 5. 749 which Spenser has in mind when he calls the Hours the porters of heaven's gate: ". . . self-moving groaned upon their hinges the gates of heaven whereof the Hours are warders, to whom is committed great heaven and Olympus, whether to throw open the thick cloud or set it to." Homer authorizes Spenser also in making them allot the seasons. See *Od.* 10. 469.

HYACINTHUS. — F. Q. 3. 6. 45; 3. 11. 37.

The untimely fate of this youth, " Phœbus paramoure And dearest love," is pathetically told by Ovid (*Met.* 10. 162 ff.). While playing at quoits with the god, Hyacinthus is struck by a discus and killed. Phœbus, in token of his grief and remembrance, causes the hyacinth, an emblem of mourning with the ancients, to spring from the blood of this beloved youth.

In the second passage Spenser says that Hyacinthus was transformed to a paunce, or pansy — a statement for which there is no classical authority.

HYDRA. — F. Q. 6. 12. 32.

Among the monstrosities which, according to Hesiod, were the offspring of Typhaon and Echidna, was the Hydra. While Spenser says that the Hydra had a thousand heads, Hyginus (*Fab.* 30) and Apollodorus (2. 5. 2) say that there were nine; Diodorus Siculus, one hundred; Virgil (*Æn.* 8. 300) describes the monster, in a general way, as "many-headed." The killing of this monster was the second labor of Hercules. See **Hercules**.

HYLAS. — F. Q. 3. 12. 7.

The incident here referred to occurred upon the journey of the Argonauts to Colchis. Hylas was a favorite of Hercules, who, when the Argo anchored upon the coast of Mysia, went to draw water from a fountain, into which he was himself drawn by the nymphs, who had been charmed by his beauty. Hercules sought him in vain, calling his name again and again, but only the echo of it replied. This echo, which is often referred to by the poets, is accounted for by Antoninus Liberalis (*Hylas*) as being really Hylas himself, who had been changed into an echo by the nymphs — they being fearful lest Hercules should discover his beloved in their fountain. See **Argonautic Expedition**.

HYLLUS. — F. Q. 4. 10. 27.

Spenser doubtless means to say Hylas, between whom and Hercules there was the closest friendship. See **Hylas**.

HYMEN. — F. Q. 1. 1. 48; V. G. 50; Ep. *passim*.

Hymen was the god of marriage, and therefore appropriately invoked in the *Epithalamion*. From among the classics, the *Epithalamium* of Catullus, written in celebration of the nuptials of Manlius and Julia, may be cited as an example: there Hymen is called upon again and again as the god of marriage, and Spenser imitates the *Io Hymen Hymenæe* in F. Q. 1. 1. 48 and in his *Epithalamion*. The custom of crowning Hymen with a garland at marriage festivals is referred to by Catullus, as by Spenser (*Ep.* 256).

HYPERION. — Mui. 51.

Helios, the sun, is here called "Hyperion's fierie childe." Hesiod (*Theog.* 134, 371 ff.), Apoll. (1. 2. 2), Diod. Sic. (5. 67. 1), may be quoted as authorities on this point. Hyperion was the child of Heaven and Earth, and, in turn, became the father of the Sun, the Moon, and the Dawn-goddess. In *V. G.* 20 the name is used for the sun itself. Compare *Met.* 8. 565

HYPONEO. — F. Q. 4. 11. 51. See **Nereids**.

HYPSIPHYLE. — F. Q. 2. 10. 56. See **Argonautic Expedition**.

INACHUS. — T. M. 447.

In the passage before us Calliope asks: —

> What oddes twixt Irus and old Inachus,
> 'Twixt best and worst, when both alike are dedd;
> If none of neither mention should make,
> Nor out of dust their memories awake?

The first of the two extremes of society here cited is Irus, the beggar of Ithaca, a characterization of whom opens the eighteenth book of the *Odyssey*.

The other character, with whom Irus is contrasted, is the celebrated river-god and hero of Argos, the first ruler of that country. Thus Euripides (*Elec.* 1) addresses him as the ancient glory of Argos, and in *Sup.* 371 Argos is called the land of Inachus. See also *Æn.* 7. 286, where the expression "Inachian Argos" occurs.

In writing the passage in question, Spenser seems to have had in mind Horace, *Carm.* 2. 3: —

> Divesne, prisco natus ab Inacho
> Nil interest an pauper et infima
> De gente sub divo moreris,
> Victima nil miserantis Orci.

See also **Sea-Gods**.

INO. — F. Q. 4. 11. 13; 5. 8. 47.

Ino is mentioned as the mother of Palæmon. She is further described as "raging," and engaged in the act of throwing her husband's murdered infant out. For the details of this tragic story,

— the madness of Athamas, the husband of Ino, and his pursuit of Ino to the brink of the sea, where she casts herself and her child, Palæmon, into the waves, — see *Met.* 4. 417 ff.; *Fast.* 6. 528.

IOLE. — F. Q. 5. 5. 24. See **Hercules.**

IPHIMEDIA. — F. Q. 3. 11. 42.

Neptune became by her the father of Otus and Ephialtes. See *Met.* 6. 115; *Od.* 11. 305; *Apoll.* 1. 7. 4.

IRIS. — F. Q. 3. 11. 47; Mui. 93.

Although Iris was originally the personification of the rainbow itself, and is sometimes identified with it in the ancient poets, she is generally considered (as in Spenser) as having an individuality apart from it. She is the messenger of the gods, particularly of Juno; and the rainbow is either the path over which she glides, or the varicolored robe in which she is clothed. *Æn.* 5. 604 ff.; *Met.* 14. 830 ff.; 1. 271; 11. 585 ff., may be cited as typical passages on this point. For the parentage of Iris, see **Thaumas.**

IRUS. — T. M. 447. See **Inachus.**

ISIS. — F. Q. 5. 7. 3 ff.

This entire passage, which describes the attributes and worship of the Egyptian divinities, Isis and Osiris, is based upon Plutarch's *Isis and Osiris*. Spenser, however, does not feel himself at all bound by the original, but follows it at times afar off. Thus he says the priests wore their hair long, while Plutarch says their heads were shaved. The interpretation of the crocodile, also, which he gives in Stanza 22, is not authorized by the original. The other points which Spenser cites, — the justice of Osiris when king of Egypt; the equity attributed to Isis; the linen garb of the priests; the crescent miters; the interpretation of Osiris as the sun, and Isis as the moon; the continence of the priests; their abstinence from fleshly food; the reason why they did not drink wine, — all these are consistent with the account given by Plutarch.

ISSA. — F. Q. 3. 11. 39.

Spenser here makes the statement that Apollo was in love with Issa, the daughter of Admetus, and it was for her sake that he fed the flocks of Admetus. There is a confusion here: *Met.* 6. 124, the evident source of this passage, says that as a shepherd, Phœbus deceived Isse, the daughter of Macareus; and with this statement Spenser has confused the more conspicuous instance of Apollo's becoming a shepherd in the service of Admetus. See **Apollo**.

ITYS. — V. G. 51.

For an explanation of this passage, see *Met.* 6. 412 ff., where it appears that the two Pandionian maids were Procne and Philomela, daughters of Pandion. The Thracian king was Tereus. He married Procne, by whom he became the father of Itys. He afterwards fell in love with Philomela; and, having deceived her, he cut out her tongue, and placed her in confinement, pretending to Procne that she was dead. Philomela, however, found means to acquaint her sister with her distress; Procne delivered her from her captivity; and together they wreaked vengeance upon the faithless Tereus by killing the boy Itys. After this a general metamorphosis took place: Procne and Philomela were changed, in their flight, to the swallow and the nightingale, respectively, while Tereus became the lapwing.

IULUS. — F. Q. 3. 9. 43. See **Æneas**.

IXION. — F. Q. 1. 5. 35; 7. 6. 29.

The presumption of Ixion in daring to aspire to the favor of Juno, and his subsequent punishment in the Lower World, are here cited. Hyginus (*Fab.* 62) and Lucian (*Dial. Deor.* 6) relate both the transgression and its punishment. Both Juno and Orpheus in their visits to the Lower World (*Met.* 4. 461; 10. 42) saw Ixion bound to his wheel, and he is mentioned as among the shades noticed by Æneas (*Æn.* 6. 601).

IXIONE. — V. G. 62. See **Hesione**.

JANUS. — F. Q. 4. 10. 12; Am. 4.

Ovid (*Fast.* 1, *passim*) has furnished a fertile source of information in regard to Janus, his double face, and his gate. Ovid's invocation of the god begins thus: —

O, Janus, thou of the two heads! origin of the year silently rolling on, thou who alone of the gods above dost behold thy own back, be thou propitious to our princes, etc.

Further: —

For the month of Janus is first, because the gate is at the very entrance.

And again: —

But, O Janus, thou of the double form, what kind of deity shall I pronounce thee to be? for Greece has no divinity corresponding to thee. Do thou, at the same time, declare the reason why thou alone of all the inhabitants of heaven lookest upon that which is behind thee, and that which is before thee.

Janus gives the reason of his shape in these words: —

Every gate has two fronts, one on either side, of which the one looks out upon the people, but the other looks inward upon the household shrine; and as the gate-keeper among you mortals, sitting near the threshold of the front of the building, sees both the goings out and the comings in, so do I, the doorkeeper of the vestibule of heaven, at the same time look forth upon the regions of the east and the west.

JASON.— F. Q. 2. 12. 44. See Argonautic Expedition.

JOVE.

Spenser is not exactly consistent in regard to the parentage of Jove: in *F. Q.* 1. 5. 22 he is called the eldest born of Night. Wishing to make Night seem as ancient as possible, Spenser makes her the parent even of Jove. In *F. Q.* 7. 6. 2 he calls Jove the son of Saturn, or Cronus.

The first passage is to be freely interpreted in the light of a line in one of the Orphic Hymns, which refers to Night as the parent of men and gods.

The second passage is supported by the *Theogony* of Hesiod. According to that, Chaos was the origin of all; from Chaos were born Earth and Night; and from Earth, Cronus and Rhea sprang, who, in turn, became the parents of Jove and other divinities.

As to the birthplace of Jove, when Mutability (*F. Q.* 7. 7.

53) wished to prove that even Jove, like all others born in this world, was subject to herself, she says:—

> Where were ye borne? Some say in Crete by name,
> Others in Thebes, and others other-where.

There is, indeed, this disagreement among the ancients in regard to the birthplace of Jove. The commonest tradition accords with Hesiod's *Theogony*, which calls him the son of Cronus and Rhea, and his birthplace Crete. Callimachus, however, in his *Hymn to Jove*, speaks of various places as claiming to be his birthplace; and Tzet. *Lyc.* 1194 mentions Thebes among the number. See **Rhea**, also.

F. Q. 7. 7. 41 represents December as riding on the goat wherewith Jove was nourished by the Idæan maid. This allusion to Jove, also, is part of the myth concerning the Cretan Zeus. According to Ovid (*Fast.* 5. 121 ff.) the Idæan maid was "Nais Amalthea, Cretæa nobilis Ida;" and the goat which nourished Jupiter was placed, in token of reward, in the sky, thus becoming the constellation of the she-goat. Other writers say that Amalthea was the name of the goat.

Great as was the power of Jove, he himself was, nevertheless, subject to the wiles of Cupid (see *F. Q.* 3. 6. 22; 3. 11. 30; 3. 11. 35; *Co. Cl.* 809; *Am.* 39); and, although married to Juno, he was the hero of numerous amours with both goddesses and mortal women. Among those who excited the love of Jove, Spenser mentions Ægina (*F. Q.* 3. 11. 35); Alcmena (*F. Q.* 3. 11. 33); *M. H. T.* 1299; *Ep.* 328); Antiope (*F. Q.* 3. 11. 35); Asteria (*F. Q.* 3. 11. 34); Danae (*F. Q.* 3. 11. 31); Europa (*F. Q.* 3. 11. 30; 5. Int. 5; 7. 7. 33; *Mui.* 278 ff.); Helle (*F. Q.* 3. 11. 30); Leda (*F. Q.* 3. 11. 32; *Pro.* 42); Maia (*Ep.* 307); Mnemosyne (*F. Q.* 3. 11. 35; 4. 11. 10); Semele (*F. Q.* 3. 11. 33); Thracian maid (*F. Q.* 3. 11. 35). For a discussion of these points, see the several headings.

The rape of Ganymede, whom Spenser refers to as the Trojan boy (*F. Q.* 3. 11. 34; 3. 12. 7) is the subject of a favorite myth with the ancients. That Jove was charmed with the beauty of Ganymede, and that in the form of an eagle he snatched him away and bore him to Olympus, where, much against the will of Juno, he became the cup-bearer of the gods, is briefly stated by Ovid (*Met.* 10. 155). The myth forms also the groundwork of two of Lucian's dialogues.

Jove became the father of numerous children. From among these, Spenser cites Cupid, calling him the offspring of Jove and Venus (*F. Q.* 1. Int. 3). See **Cupid**.

Spenser further mentions Cynthia (*F. Q.* 7. 7. 50), who was especially beloved by Jove; Hercules (*Ep.* 328); Mars (*R. R.* 11); Phoebus (*V. G.* 2); the Graces (*F. Q.* 6. 10. 22); the Hours (*F. Q.* 7. 7. 45; *Ep.* 99); the Litæ (*F. Q.* 5. 9. 31); the Muses (*F. Q.* 4. 11. 10; *S. C.* June 66; *R. T.* 369). For a discussion of these, see the several headings.

Besides those above mentioned, there are references to the "twins of Jove" in *F. Q.* 5. Int. 6; *Pro.* 173. These are Castor and Pollux. (See **Leda**.) The circumstances of their transference to the sky under the name of the Gemini are related by Ovid (*Fast.* 700 ff.) and Hyginus (*Poet. Astron.* 2. Gemini).

Spenser further declares the Water-nymphs to be of Jove's "kinde." For an explanation of this, see **Nereids**.

Jove won and maintained his supremacy only at the expense of two famous contests, — the first with the Titans, the second with the Giants; for, although confounded by ancient writers and by Spenser himself, these two contests were originally quite distinct.

The Titans, we are told by Hesiod, were the children of Uranus and Gea, and were called Titans (from τιταίνω) by their father, because they stretched forth their hands in violence against him. After the Titans had gained the power, and had placed Cronus, one of their number, upon the throne of their father, they, in turn, were assailed by Jove. Hesiod (*Theog.* 616 ff.) relates in a vivid manner the story of this contest, when earth and sea and sky shared in the general upheaval. Jove in the end came off victorious; and the Titans were hurled from their heavenly abodes and condemned to Tartarus, though their descendants continued to inhabit the earth. Spenser refers to this war in *F. Q.* 7. 6. 2, and 7. 6. 27. In *F. Q.* 3. 7. 47, and 5. 1. 9 he employs the name Titans to designate the Giants — instances of the confusion referred to above.

The famous contest of Jove with the earth-born giants, who were so rash as to assail even heaven itself, is related at some length by Apollodorus (1. 6. 1 ff.) and Claudian (*Gigant.*) and frequently referred to by others among the ancients. Besides the references to this point already quoted, Spenser mentions the rebellion of the Giants in *F. Q.* 2. 10. 3; 5. 7. 10; *R. R.* 4 and 12.

The adjective "Phlegræan," which is used in the first two of these references, is explained in the light of Apoll. 1. 6. 1; Claud. *Gigant.* 4; Diod. Sic. 4. 21. 5; 5. 71. 4: it was in Phlegra in Italy, the home of the Giants, that the contest took place. See also **Apollo**.

Spenser further relates that under the wrathful power of Earth, the mother of the slain, the blood of the Giants which was shed on this occasion became wine — the liquor that has "the mindes of men with fury fraught." This idea is from Plutarch's *Isis* and *Osiris*.

The picture which Spenser gives us of Jove is made up of bits of mosaic, — a passage here and an epithet there. When, however, these bits are pieced together, we have the Jove of the *Iliad*.

Perhaps no passage of that poem more clearly shows the relation of Jove to the other gods than his own address to them on Mt. Olympus, which opens the eighth book of the *Iliad*. With this passage may be compared *F. Q.* 5. 7. 1, where Jove is described as one "who doth true justice deale To his inferior Gods."

When, according to *Iliad* 15. 187 ff., the universe was partitioned among the three sons of Saturn, **Jupiter** was allotted "the wide heaven, in clear air and clouds." Hence Spenser calls him the ruler of day and night (*F. Q.* 1. 5. 42), and the day and the stars his lamps (see *F. Q.* 1. 5. 19; 1. 7. 23; 3. 1. 57; 3. 4. 51).

According to the *Iliad*, the abode of Jove is on the top of Mt. Olympus, in the heavens, whence he rules the world. With this conception compare *F. Q.* 1. 4. 11; 1. 4. 17; 7. 6. 15.

Homer frequently describes Jove as thundering; and Spenser follows him in such passages as *F. Q.* 1. 5. 42; 2. 6. 10; 2. 6. 50;

4. 5. 37. With his thunderbolts he killed Phaeton, and thrust Æsculapius down to hell. See **Æsculapius** and **Phaeton**.

A storm was supposed to be expressive of his anger. On this point compare *F. Q.* 1. 1. 6; 1. 8. 9; 4. 6. 14 with the forceful description of a storm as expressive of the wrath of Jove against the injustice of men in *Il.* 16. 384 ff.

With the peculiar description in the first of these passages, compare Lucret. 1. 251: —

>... pereunt imbres, ubi eos pater Æther
> In gremium matris Terræ præcipitavit.

Throughout the *Iliad*, Jove appears as the arbiter of justice to gods and men. His rewards are great and his punishments fearful. Thus Spenser represents him (*F. Q.* 4. 3. 44) as advancing the worthy to heaven, as in the case of Hercules and many others (Hyg. *Fab.* 225), and in condemning the damned to Phlegethon (*F. Q.* 1. 5. 33). He punishes Prometheus for his audacity (*F. Q.* 2. 10. 70), on which point see **Prometheus**. He is also the judge in the contest between Pallas and Neptune over the naming of Athens (*Mui.* 305 ff.). See **Arachne**. In *F. Q.* 1. 5. 25 Spenser follows *Il.* 8. 19, and speaks of the chain of necessity — the concatenation of cause and effect — "Which fast is tyde to Jove's eternall seat."

While the Homeric Jove is always superior to Fate, Spenser says: —

> Not so; for what the Fates do once decree,
> Not all the gods can change, nor Jove himself can free.
> *F. Q.* 4. 2. 51.

This conception of Jove and the other gods as limited in power by the Fates is rather in accord with such passages as *Met.* 15. 781, 807 ff.

The bird of Jove referred to in *F. Q.* 2. 11. 43; *R. R.* 17; *V. W.* V. 4, is the eagle. With these passages compare the opening lines of that famous ode by Horace, which records the triumphs of Drusus (*Carm.* 4. 4): —

> Like the fierce bird with thunder-laden wing, etc.

In *F. Q.* 2. 5. 31; *V. B.* 5 we have a reference to the tree that was sacred to Jove. This is the oak, through whose rustling leaves the god was supposed to make his will known at his oracle at Dodona (*Od.* 19. 296).

The great image of Jove "in Olympus [!] placed" (*R. R.* 2) is the famous statue of the god at Olympia in Elis. It was the work of Phidias, and was considered to be one of the wonders of the ancient world (Hyg. *Fab.* 223).

In *V. W. V.* 11 Jove is called the patron of the Capitol at Rome. This epithet, more briefly expressed by the Romans in the title of Capitolinus, has reference to the fact that Jupiter had a temple upon the Capitoline Hill at Rome (*Fast.* 2. 69).

The Jupiter of the Greeks and Romans was identified with the Egyptian Ammon, to whom there is a single reference in Spenser (*F. Q.* 1. 5. 48). The "mightie monarch" of this passage is Alexander, who was first hailed by the Egyptian priests as the son of Zeus Ammon. For an explanation of this, see Plutarch. See also Lucian, *Dial. Mort.* 12; 13; 14.

A fitting close to this article is the *Hom. Hymn to Jove*, which sums up many of the points here alluded to: —

> Jove now I sing; the greatest and the best
> Of all those powers that are with deity blest;
> That far-off doth his dreadful voice diffuse;
> And, being king of all, doth all conduce
> To all their ends; who (shut from all gods else
> With Themis, that the laws of all things tells)
> Their fit composures to their times doth call,
> Weds them together, and preserves this all.
> Grace then, O far-heard Jove! the grace thou'st given;
> Most glorious, and most great, of earth and heaven.

JUNO.

Spenser's references to Juno are slight and few in number. In *F. Q.* 7. 7. 26 (a part of the paraphrase of Ovid's presentation of the Pythagorean philosophy of change), after naming the four elements, — earth, water, air, and fire, — Spenser says that Juno is ruler of the air. In making this statement, Spenser follows Macrobius, *Sat.* 1. 5, where Juno is called *aeris arbitra*, an epithet arising from the fact that the early Romans identified Juno with the moon, which sails through the air.

In *Ep.* 390 ff, Juno is invoked as the patron of marriage,

and the divinity who presides over childbirth. The origin of the first of these ideas is in the wifely relation which Juno bore to Jove; her interest in offspring arises from the fact that she first made Saturn a parent — that is, she was his eldest child (see *Fast.* 6. 26 ff., where she is frequently alluded to as the guardian of marriage, as in Ap. Rh. 4. 96; *Æn.* 4. 166.)

The character of Juno (or Hera), as represented by the ancients from Homer down, is distinguished by jealousy, arrogance, and a spirit of contention and revenge. Lucian, in his Dialogues, portrays these characteristics in a most realistic manner, and makes of the queen of heaven a mortal among mortals.

The fickleness of Jove tended to develop the vengeful side of Juno's nature, and we frequently find her engaged in some scheme for thwarting his amours. Thus Spenser refers to her anger against Latona (*F. Q.* 2. 12. 13), and to the deception which she practiced on Semele (*F. Q.* 3. 11. 3), for which see **Latona** and **Semele**.

In *F. Q.* 1. 4. 17 we have a picture of the famous golden chariot of Juno, drawn by peacocks. While this passage was, no doubt, suggested indirectly by *Il.* 5. 720 — where the chariot is described as golden in part, though drawn, not by peacocks, but by horses — the direct source of Spenser's description is *Met.* 2. 5. 31 ff., where the variegated birds are mentioned.

The "ey-spotted traine" of Juno's bird is referred to in *Mui.* 95. For the source of this, see **Argus**.

LACHESIS. — F. Q. 4. 2. 48. See **Fates**.

LAERTES. — V. G. 67. See **Ulysses**.

LAOMEDIA. — F. Q. 4. 11. 51. See **Nereids**.

LAOMEDON. — F. Q. 2. 11. 19. See **Apollo**.

LAPITHÆ. — F. Q. 4. 1. 23; 6. 10. 13; V. G. 6.

These passages all refer to the bloody contest between the Lapithæ and the Centaurs at the marriage of Pirithous, one of the Lapithæ, and Hippodamia. On this occasion Eurytus, one of the Centaurs, made an attempt upon the bride, and a bloody fray ensued. Compare *Met.* 12. 210 ff. See also **Ariadne**.

LATINUS. — F. Q. 3. 9. 42; 3. 9. 43.

Latinus was the king of Latium at the time Æneas and his followers reached the country. It was decreed by unmistakable signs that Æneas should marry Lavinia, the only daughter of Latinus, and that thus the two peoples should be united; but the oracle was fulfilled only after bloody wars and the final defeat of Turnus, the foe and rival of Æneas. See *Æneid* 7; 8; 9; 10; 11; 12.

LATONA.

For the references to Latona as the mother of Apollo and Diana, and the circumstances attending their birth (*F. Q.* 2. 12. 13; 6. 2. 25; *V. G.* 2), see **Apollo**.

For the references to the wrath which Latona's children visited upon the hapless Niobe (*F. Q.* 5. 10. 7; *S. C.* Apr. 86), see **Niobe**.

The single remaining passage (*V. G.* 48) refers to the punishment of Tityus for his assault upon Latona, for which see **Tityus**.

LEANDER. — H. L. 231.

The romantic love of Hero and Leander is here referred to. Every night Leander of Abydos swam the Hellespont (not the Euxine waves) in order to reach his beloved Hero, a priestess of Venus, upon Sestus, in which undertaking he finally perished. The source of this reference is, no doubt, the poem of *Hero and Leander*, by Musæus.

LEDA. — F. Q. 3. 11. 32; Pro. 43.

Jove's intrigue with Leda, whom he approached in the shape of a swan, is referred to in these passages, in support of which see *Met.* 6. 109 and Apoll. 3. 10. 7.

Castor and Pollux were the offspring of this union. Their constellation, the Gemini, is referred to in *F. Q.* 7. 7. 34; *R. T.* 386. For the origin of this constellation as explained by Ovid, see *Fast.* 5. 697 ff.

LETHE. — F. Q. 1. 3. 36; S. C. March 23; R. T. 428; V. G. 43.

"Lethe is a lake in hell, which the poetes call the lake of forgetfulness." — E. K., Glosse, *S. C.* March 23.

Compare *Æn.* 6. 714, where Lethe is described as a river of the Lower World, whose waters dispelled care and produced oblivion in those shades who were destined to be reincarnated.

For *R. T.* 428, see **Thetis**.

LIAGORE.— F. Q. 3. 4. 41. See Apollo.

LIAGORE.— F. Q. 4. 11. 51. See Nereids.

LINUS.— R. T. 383.

Linus is here mentioned as a poet in close connection with Orpheus. They both belong to the number of those half-mythical and half-historical poets who were believed to have been under the immediate instruction of Apollo and the Muses. Their shadowy personalities haunt the pages of classic literature, and in later times they came to be regarded as historical characters.

Apollodorus (2. 3. 9) declares Linus and Orpheus to have been brothers, the sons of the Muse Calliope and Œagrus (1. 3. 2). Virgil (*Ecl.* 4. 56) speaks of Calliope and Apollo as their parents.

Diodorus Siculus says that Linus invented the lichanos (3. 59. 6) and measure and song (3. 67. 1); and that among his pupils were Hercules, Thamyris, and Orpheus, the first of whom struck and killed his master with his lyre. He adds that Linus left behind him certain works committed to writing (3. 67. 2).

LISIANASSA.— F. Q. 4. 11. 50. See **Nereids**.

LITÆ.— F. Q. 5. 9. 31.

This name is a personification of the Greek word for "prayers" (λιταί), as in *Iliad* 9. 502 ff.— a passage which is the source of the general conception here expressed. With Homer, as with Spenser, they are daughters of Jove, who attend their father as mediators between him and man; and they bend the wills of mortals also. But while Homer describes them as "halting and wrinkled and of eyes askance, that have their task withal to go in the steps of Sin," Spenser says they are fair virgins and lovely daughters. Moreover, Homer mentions no particular number of Litæ; neither does he give their names or that of their mother. Spenser, on the other hand, calls them the daughters of Jove and Themis (the personification of justice), and gives their names as Dice, Eunomie, and Irene, in which particulars he is following Hesiod in his designation of the Hours.

This fusion of the Litæ with the Hours is arbitrary on the part of our poet: it may have been suggested, however, by the ethical conception of the Hours, which is evident in Hesiod (*Theog.* 901 ff.) and Pindar (*Olymp.* 13). It is clear, from the names themselves, that the Hours of Hesiod are something more than those of Homer, who represents them as divinities of the seasons only: with Hesiod there is an ethical conception, and they administer justice, good laws, and peace to men, as their names indicate. This idea held its own as time went on, as will be seen from the passage by Pindar, referred to above: "For therein dwell Order, and her sisters, sure foundation of states, Justice and like-minded Peace, dispensers of wealth to men, wise Themis' golden daughters."

This conception, however, is so different from that of Homer concerning the Litæ that, as said above, it could not have done more than suggest to Spenser the fusion of the two.

LUCINA. — F. Q. 2. 1. 53; 3. 6. 27.

This was a name given to both Juno and Diana as the goddesses who preside at childbirth. See *Fast.* 2. 449 ff., where the name as applied to Diana is derived from *lucus*, a grove, or (more probably) from *lux, lucis*, meaning light; for she it is who brings children to the light. See also *Fast.* 3. 255.

LYÆUS. — F. Q. 3. 1. 51.

The derivation of this name, Λυαῖος, from the verb λύω, *to loose* or *deliver*, shows the appropriateness of it as an epithet of Bacchus, the god of care-dispelling wine. See *Anac.* 6. 8. 24, 25, 53; *Anth. Lat.* 745.

MÆNADES. — F. Q. 5. 8. 47.

The fury of the Mænades, or priestesses of Bacchus, is here referred to, with which compare Eurip. *Bacchanals, passim.*

MAIA.
> Flora now calleth forth eche flower,
> And bids make readie Maias bower,
> That newe is upryst from bedde.
> S. C. Mar. 17.

E. K., commenting upon this passage, says: "*Maias bower*, that is, the pleasaunt field, or rather the Maye bushes. Maia is a goddess, and the mother of Mercurie, in honour of whome the moneth of Maye is of her name so called, as sayth Macrobius."

With this authority compare *F. Q.* 4. 3. 42; 7. 6. 16; *M. H. T.* 1257.

In *Ep.* 307 Spenser names Tempe as the place where Jove and Maia met, but his authority is not evident.

MARS.

The Mars of Spenser's poems appears under two different aspects, — as delighting in war, and as conquered by love. As the god of war Mars (Ares) appears often in the *Iliad*, and the *Hom. Hymn to Mars* gives us a clear idea of his warlike character. Compare *F Q.* 1. 11. 7; *S. C.* Oct. 39.

In *R. R.* 11, the warlike Roman people are spoken of as the offspring of Mars. Macrobius tells that the Romans worshiped Mars under the title of "Marspiter," that is, *Father Mars* (*Sat.* 1. 19. 3).

This fact is easily explained in the light of the myth which makes Mars the father of Romulus, the founder of the Roman state (*Fast.* 3. 1 ff.). The month of March was sacred to him, and he was second only to Jupiter among the Roman people.

But there is a hint in *F. Q.* 1. Int. 3 that Mars could at times lay aside his fierce aspect: —

> . . . and with you bring triumphant Mart,
> In loves and gentle jollities arraid,
> After his murdrous spoyles and bloudie rage allayd.

In *F. Q.* 2. 6. 35 Spenser goes so far as to declare that —

> . . . Mars is Cupidoes frend,
> And is for Venus loves renowmed more
> Then all his wars and spoiles, the which he did of yore.

This is a reference to the love of Venus and Mars, which was disclosed by Phœbus. It is the theme of the bard in the eighth book of the *Odyssey*. See also *F. Q.* 2. 6. 35; 3. 6. 24; 3. 11. 36; 3. 11. 44.

The planet Mars is cited in *F. Q.* 5. Int. 8; 7. 7. 52; *Am.* 60. See Hyg. *Poet. Astron.* 2. De quinque stellis; 4. De Marte.

MEDEA. — *F. Q.* 2. 12. 44; 5. 8. 47. See **Argonautic** Expedition.

MEDUSA. — F. Q. 3. 11. 42; R. T. 647.

In both these passages Medusa is referred to as the mother of Pegasus, the winged horse; in the first, as among those who won the love of Neptune, by whom she became the mother of Pegasus.

Apollodorus (2. 4. 3) and Ovid (*Met.* 6. 119) say that Medusa was the mother of the horse by Neptune, which authors Spenser follows. It should be added, however, that while Ovid says that Neptune deceived Medusa in the shape of a bird, Spenser says that it was as a winged horse — a slight deviation, for which there is apparently no classical authority.

The reference to her snaky locks is explained by *Met.* 4. 790 ff.: it was in the temple of Minerva that Neptune and Medusa met, and the goddess punished such desecration by changing the beautiful hair of Medusa to snaky locks.

MEGÆRA. — T. M. 164.

One of the three Furies, mentioned by Virgil (*Æn.* 12. 846). The daughters of Night, made hideous with serpents and provided with swift wings, they strike terror to the hearts of mortals.

MELITE. — F. Q. 4. 11. 49. See Nereids.

MELPOMENE. — S. C. Nov. 53. See Muses.

MENIPPE. — F. Q. 4. 11. 51. See Nereids.

MERCURY.

Spenser alludes to the messenger of the gods under the names of Hermes, Mercury, and the son of Maia.

For the parentage of Mercury (*F. Q.* 4. 3. 42; 7. 6. 16; *M. H. T.* 1257), see **Maia**.

In *F. Q.* 7. 6. 16 ff.; *M. H. T.* 1257, Mercury appears as a messenger. In *F. Q.* 2. 12. 41 there is a reference to his rod, —

> With which he wonts the Stygian realmes invade
> Through ghostly horror and eternall shade:
> Th' infernall feends with it he can asswage,
> And Orcus tame, whome nothing can persuade,
> And rule the Furyes when they most doe rage.

In *F. Q.* 4. 3. 42, to this rod is compared one which is wound with two serpents, crowned with an olive garland. In

M. H. T. 1292 the power of Mercury's caduceus in bringing about continuous night at the time of Jupiter's intrigue with Alcmena is referred to. In *R. T.* 665 and *M. H. T.* 1257 the wings of Mercury are mentioned.

Numerous passages from the *Iliad* and other writings might be quoted to prove that Mercury was the messenger of the gods, a fact which is playfully brought out in Lucian *Dial. Deor.* 24, where Hermes grumbles over the numerous demands made upon him.

His magic staff also is mentioned in the *Iliad*; and, in the *Hom. Hymn to Mercury*, we learn that it was the gift of Apollo. There is, however, no mention of the serpents until later times. Hyginus (*Poet. Astron.* 2. 7), accounting for their presence on the staff, says that Mercury one day came across two serpents fighting one with the other. He extended his rod between them and they separated. The rod, in consequence, became a token of peace, and it was represented as adorned with two intertwined serpents. Spenser, as if to emphasize the idea of peace, adds an olive crown; and there is a certain consistency in this, since by some the olive-tree was believed to be the gift of Mercury and not of Minerva (Diod. Sic. 1. 16. 2).

The power of this staff in calming certain creatures in Hades is brought out by Spenser in the above-quoted passage. There is a somewhat similar general statement in *Æn.* 4. 242 ff.; Lucian *Dial. Deor.* 7. For a particular instance, see *Od.* 24. 1 ff., where Homer describes Mercury conducting the souls of the suitors to the Lower World. See also Lucian, *Dial. Mort. passim*.

For the power of Mercury's caduceus at the time of Jove's intrigue with Alcmena, see *Il.* 24. 343, where to Mercury is attributed the power of granting or withholding sleep by the exercise of his wand.

Although Mercury is generally represented as with wings, all writers do not agree in placing the wings: some make them an adornment of his hat; others, of his staff; while others, like Spenser, place them upon his feet. With Spenser compare *Æn.* 4. 239. It is, of course, more than probable that Spenser was indebted to works of art also for his conception of Mercury and his attributes.

F. Q. 7. 6. 14, and 7. 7. 51 refer to Mercury as a planet. Spenser follows the Ptolemaic system when, in the first of these passages, he says that Mercury "next [to the moon] doth raigne."

MINERVA. — Mui. 273. See Arachne

MINOS. — V. G. 78.

One of the judges in the Lower World: "Minos rules the scrutiny, and shakes the urn; he convokes the conclave of the silent dead, and learns their lives, and the charges brought against them." — *Æn.* 6. 432 ff.

MNEMOSYNE. — F. Q. 3. 11. 35.

Spenser is again indebted to the list of Jove's transformations mentioned by Ovid. See *Met.* 6. 114. Mnemosyne is referred to in the other passages as Memory, for which see **Muses**.

MŒNADES. — F. Q. 5. 8. 47. See Mænades.

MORPHEUS.

When Archimago sends one of his legions of sprites to the house of Morpheus to obtain from the god of sleep "A fit false dreame, that can delude the sleepers sent" (*F. Q.* 1. 1. 38 ff.), he is simply following Juno, who sent Iris to the god of sleep with a similar request — that he would dispatch a dream to Halcyone, telling her of the death of her husband Ceyx (*Met.* 11. 590 ff.). A comparison of these two passages will reveal their general similarity, although in certain minor points there is a difference: thus, for instance, with Ovid, Morpheus is but one of the thousand sons of Father Sleep who, as dreams, do the bidding of their master; while, with Spenser, Morpheus himself is the god of sleep, having the dreams in his control. But the abode of sleep, its situation, the quietness pervading it, and the drowsiness of the god, are practically the same in both accounts. The twin portals of sleep are not from Ovid, however, but from Virgil (*Æn.* 6. 893 ff.; cf. *Od.* 19. 562 ff.).

The leaden mace of Morpheus (*F. Q.* 1. 4. 44) may have been suggested to our poet by the Lethe-drenched branch which the god of sleep shakes over the head of Palinurus (*Æn.* 5. 854), or perhaps by Hermes' soporific wand (*Od.* 5. 47; *Æn.* 4. 244). See also *F. Q.* 6. 8. 34; *V. B.* 15.

MUSES.

In the number and names of the Muses as given in *The Teares of the Muses*, Spenser follows the list of Hesiod (*Theog.* 77 ff.); but the distinct arts which Spenser attributes to the "sacred Sisters nine" are not mentioned by Hesiod, except in the case of Calliope, who is named as the most honored of the Muses, the one who sings of the great acts of virtuous monarchs. With Hesiod, poetry in general is the province of all the Muses, and with their master Apollo they give inspiration to the poet:—

> Bless'd whom with eyes of love the Muses view,
> Sweet flow his words, gentle as falling dew.

Spenser, however, follows later authorities, and distinguishes a special province for each of the nine:—

Clio speaks as the Muse of History, who registers noble feats, and keeps alive the memory of them from age to age. Compare *Anth. Lat.* 664.

Melpomene declares that it is her part "The Stage with Tragick buskin to adorne." Compare Hor. *Carm.* 1. 24.

Thalia boasts that she is the queen of comedy. Compare *Anth. Lat.* 664.

Euterpe speaks as the Muse of lyric poetry. Compare Hor. *Carm.* 1. 1.

Terpsichore is the Muse of the choral song and dance, who "earst in joyance did abound." Compare Plato, *Phædr.* 259 C.

Erato sings, "Love wont to be schoolmaster of my skill." Compare Plato, *Phædr.* 259 D.

Calliope, as Muse of the epic, boasts that she is the nurse of virtue, immortalizing the deeds of heroes. See above.

Urania, as Muse of astronomy, talks of the stars and her "heavenlie discipline." Compare *Anth. Lat.* 664; Plato, *Phædr.* 259 D.

Polyhymnia utters her lament in the capacity of the Muse of lofty hymns. Compare Hor. *Carm.* 1. 1.

Thus, also, in other poems, Spenser preserves the distinct offices of the several Muses: **Calliope**, *F. Q.* 7. 6. 37; **Clio**, *F. Q.* 3. 3. 4; 7. 6. 37; **Melpomene**, *S. C. Nov.* 53.

E. K., in his note on Calliope (*S. C.* Apr. 100), has in mind

Anth. Lat. 664 — a poem already cited — when he assigns to this Muse "The firste glorye of Heroical verse," and attributes to Virgil a line in regard to Polyhymnia, with which he disagrees. And again, in his note on Melpomene (*S. C.* Nov. 53), E. K. quotes from the same poem, attributing it also to Virgil: —

> Melpomene tragico proclamat mœsta boatu.

There is a discrepancy in Spenser's references to the parentage of the Muses. The passages touching upon this point are of two classes: those which refer to Jove as their father, and those which mention Apollo in that relation. See *F. Q.* 4. 11. 10; *S. C.* June 66; *R. T.* 369; and *F. Q.* 1. 11. 5; 3. 3. 4; *T. M.* 2; *Ep.* 121. Whenever the mother of the Muses is mentioned, it is Mnemosyne (Memory).

The weight of classical authority is in support of making Jove and Mnemosyne the parents of the Muses. (See *Theog.*) There seems to be very slight ground for calling Apollo their father; though his intimate connection with the Muses, as their leader, would quite naturally suggest it.

Spenser deviates from the classics in calling the Muses the sisters of Phaeton, who drove the chariot of the Sun (*T. M.* 11); and in saying that Calliope was the mother of the Palici (*T. M.* 13). See **Phaeton** and **Palici**.

Certain haunts of the Muses are especially mentioned in *T. M.*, *passim*, as elsewhere in Spenser's poems. These are the spring on Mt. Helicon (see **Pegasus**); Mt. Parnassus (especially sacred to Apollo — and therefore to the Muses — because the oracle of Delphi was at its base. See *Hom. Hymn to Apollo* (Pythian); Paus. 10. 5. 6); and the "speaking streams of pure Castalion." (Compare "Castaliæ vocalibus undis Invisus." — Stat. *Silv.* 5. 5.)

Calliope is further named in June, 57. Other general references to the Muses are too numerous to mention.

The office of the Muses is suggestively stated in the *Hom. Hymn to the Muses and Apollo:* —

> The Muses, Jove and Phœbus, now I sing:
> For from the far-off-shooting Phœbus spring
> All poets and musicians; and from Jove
> Th' ascent of kings. The man the Muses love,

> Felicity blesses; elocution's choice
> In syrup laying, of sweetest breath, his voice.
> Hail, seed of Jove, my song your honors give;
> And so, in mine, shall yours and others' live.

MYRRHA. — F. Q. 3. 2. 41. See **Adonis**.

The epithet "Arabian" is explained by the tradition that Myrrha in her flight over wide countries rested in Sabæa, in Arabia Felix (see *Met.* 10. 480). Compare Virg. *Ciris*, 237.

NAIS. — F. Q. 7. 7. 40. See **Chiron**.

NARCISSUS.

> Foolish Narcisse, that likes the **watry** shore.
> *F. Q.* 3. 6. 45.
>
> ... lyke Narcissus vaine,
> Whose eyes him starv'd.
> *Am.* 35.

The story of Narcissus, who fell in love with his own reflection in the water, and was transformed into the flower, is related in *Met.* 3. 402.

NELEUS. — F. Q. 4. 11. 14. See **Sea-Gods**.

NEMÆAN (lion). — F. Q. 5. Int. 6; 7. 7. 36; Mui. 72. See **Hercules**.

NEMERTEA. — F. Q. 4. 11. 51. See **Nereids**.

NEMESIS. — Mui. 2.

In this passage Nemesis appears as the spiteful instigator of a quarrel "Betwixt two mightie ones of great estate."

This is not in accord with the earliest classical conception of Nemesis, as the personification of a regard for what is due; but rather with the later conception of this divinity, as envious of the prosperity of mortals and of a vengeful character. Eurip. *Orest.* 1362; Soph. *Elec.* 792.

NEPENTHE. — F. Q. 4. 3. 42 ff.

The name of this magic potion is from the Greek adjective νηπενθής, *dispelling sorrow*, which is employed in *Od.* 4. 221 to describe a drug which allayed all care. Spenser is, no doubt, indebted to this passage for his description.

NEPTUNE.

"... And to me fell the hoary sea, to be my habitation for ever, when we shook the lots." Thus says Neptune (Poseidon) to Iris, when he relates the partition of the universe among Jupiter, Pluto, and himself (*Il.* 15. 187 ff.); and thus he appears in all classical literature as the god of the sea and watery elements in general. Compare *F. Q.* 1. 3. 32; 2. 6. 10; 3. 4. 10; 7. 7. 26.

Sometimes Spenser employs the name Neptune to denote a mere personification of the sea, as in *F. Q.* 3. 4. 32, where the surface of the waves is called the back of Neptune (compare *Il.* 2. 159); and in *F. Q.* 3. 4. 42, where it is designated as the neck of Neptune (compare Lucret. 2. 472).

In *F. Q.* 3. 11. 40 we have a striking and elaborate picture of the god of the seas; he is seated in a chariot drawn by four great "hippodames," and in his hand he wields a trident. In regard to the hippodames, the *Century Dictionary* may be cited in support of the probability that Spenser had in mind the hippocampus, a sea-monster on which the sea-gods, and especially Neptune, rode. See Strab. 384, and compare Philostratus 774. The trident is the familiar attribute of Neptune. The whole picture may have been suggested to our poet by *Æn.* 1. 142 ff., where the god is described as riding upon the waves in his chariot, drawn by steeds, the trident in his hand; but it is consistent with the representations of Neptune in art also. See Paus. 2. 1, a passage describing the statues before the temple of Poseidon at Corinth.

For the contest between Neptune and Minerva over the naming of Athens (*Mui.* 306 ff.), see **Arachne.**

In *F. Q.* 3. 8. 30 the mighty herd of Neptune in charge of Proteus, the shepherd of the seas, is mentioned. This passage is undoubtedly derived from those verses of the *Odyssey* (4. 384 ff.) which describe Proteus and his flock; whence it appears that the herd was composed of *phocæ*, or seals, or — as Spenser calls them farther on — *phocas.*

When the Medway and the Thames were united, an imposing marriage-feast was held in the house of Proteus, to which came a numerous company of sea-gods, with their offspring (*F. Q.* 4. 11. 8 ff.). At the head of this august procession were Neptune and his bride, the lovely Amphitrite. See **Amphitrite.**

But the affections of the variable god of the seas were not confined to one. In *F. Q.* 4. 9. 23 and 3. 11. 42, his love for Arne, the daughter of Æolus, is cited. For this and the other immediate references to the loves of Neptune, see under the several names.

The "great equipage Which from great Neptune do derive their parentage," and which are enumerated in *F. Q.* 4. 11. 13 ff., are considered under the heads of **Sea-Gods** and **Founders of Nations**.

NEREIDS.

To the wedding of the Medway and the Thames came the fifty Nereids, daughters of Nereus and Doris (*F. Q.* 4. 11. 48 ff.). In the number of these nymphs Spenser follows Hesiod, who mentions fifty (*Theog.* 243 ff.); Homer names only thirty-three (*Il.* 18. 39 ff.), and Apollodorus, forty-five (1. 2. 7). For the names, also, Spenser is indebted to Hesiod in all but two instances: in place of Thoe and Cymatolege, Spenser gives **Phao** and **Poris**, names which are not given in the lists of either Homer or Apollodorus, nor are they mentioned by any ancient author, so far as is known. They are, then, probably original with Spenser himself. The nymph Eudora of Hesiod and Apollodorus appears in Spenser as **Endore**. According to Upton this is a misprint.

In regard to the epithets employed, Spenser follows no original with exactness. While Apollodorus employs no epithets to describe the Nereids, Homer but three, and Hesiod not more than fourteen, Spenser lavishes adjectives or descriptive phrases upon all but five. The following lists will show the instances in which Spenser agrees with or varies from Hesiod in this matter:—

SPENSER.	HESIOD.
White hand Eunica	ῥοδόπηχυς
Joyous Thalia	ἐρόεσσα
Sweete Melita	χαρίεσσα
Milkewhite Galatea	εὐειδής
Speedy Hippothoe	ἐρόεσσα
And she that with her least word can asswage The surging seas, when they do sorest rage, Cymodoce,	Κυμοδόκη θ', ἥ κυματ' ἐν ἠεροειδέι πόντῳ πνοιάς τε ζαθέων ἀνέμων σὺν Κυματολήγῃ 'Ρεῖα πρηΰνει καὶ
Goodly Amphitrite	εὐσφώρῳ 'Αμφιτρίτῃ

SPENSER.	HESIOD.
And, seeming still to smile, Glauconome	φιλομμειδής
Fresh Alimeda deckt with girlond greene	εὐστέφανος
Hyponeo with salt-bedewed wrests	ῥοδόπηχυς
And Psamathe [much praised] for her brode snowy brests	χαρίεσσα δέμας
And she that virtue loves and vice detests, Euarna	φυήν τ' ἐρατὴ καὶ εἶδος ἄμωμος
Menippe true in trust	δίη
And Nemertea learned well to rule her lust.	ἣ πατρὸς ἔχει νόον ἀθανάτοιο.

After summing up the Nereids (*F. Q.* 4. 11. 52) Spenser says: —

> And yet, besides, three thousand more there were
> Of th' Oceans seede, but Joves and Phœbus kinde;
> The which in floods and fountains doe appere,
> And all mankinde do nourish with their waters clere.

That is, he means to say that although the native element of these nymphs is the water, yet in their rank and character they are associated with Zeus and Apollo. In support of this may be cited such passages as *Il.* 20. 8, where the nymphs are represented as present at one of the Olympic assemblies with Zeus and the other gods; also, on account of the prophetic power which certain fountains were supposed to confer on those who drank of them, the nymphs who inhabited them were regarded as endowed with oracular power. Thus is Spenser justified in saying that they are of the same nature with Phœbus. In support of this see Paus. 4. 27.

NEREIS.— V. G. 71.

A patronymic from Nereus, one of the Nereids, daughters of Nereus.

NEREUS.

This sea-god is called by our poet "th' eldest and the best" of the children of Ocean and Tethys (*F. Q.* 4. 11. 18), and is further described as possessed of an upright character, and endowed with the gift of prophecy. This passage is an amplification of *Theog.* 233 ff.; although Hesiod says that Nereus was born of Ocean and Earth, rather than of Ocean and Tethys, who were the parents of numerous rivers, and so considered by Spenser in this passage. It appears from Hesiod that Nereus was the firstborn of his parents, and was respected for his wise moderation, an indirect allusion to his prophetic genius. Horace devotes one of his odes to the prophecy of Nereus concerning the fall of Troy (*Carm.* 1. 15), and other cases of his foretelling the future might be mentioned.

Nereus became by Doris the father of fifty Nereids (*F. Q.* 4. 11. 52), among whom is mentioned Thetis, as also in *V. G.* 62. See **Doris** and **Nereids**.

In *F. Q.* 3. 4. 19 he is mentioned as the father of Cymoent.

As a god of the sea, he appears in *V. B.* 13, and in *F. Q.* 1. 3. 31, the grateful sailor, safe returned to port, crowns the god with cups.

NESÆA.—F. Q. 4. 11. 49. See **Nereids**.

NESO.—F. Q. 4. 11. 50. See **Nereids**.

NICTILEUS.—V. G. 22. See **Nyctelius**.

NINUS. — F. Q. 1. 5. 48; 2. 9. 21; 2. 9. 56; R. T. 511.

Ninus and his wife Semiramis, the reputed founders of the Assyrian empire, must be regarded as mythical characters. Diodorus Siculus (2. 1 ff.) relates the numerous wars of this king; his conquests were so great that Spenser is warranted in saying that he was "of all the world obeyed."

Diodorus says Semiramis was the founder of Babylon (*tower of Babel*, Spenser) but the achievements of Ninus and his wife are so closely connected as to warrant Spenser in attributing this work to Ninus. Diodorus mentions the Assyrian bitumen abounding in the region around Babylon, of which the walls of the city were built. Spenser, it will be noticed, somewhat carelessly calls this "Ægyptian slime."

NIOBE.—F. Q. 4. 7. 30; 5. 10. 7; S. C. Apr. 87.

These passages may all be explained in the light of *Met.* 6. 146 ff., which relates that Niobe, the mother of seven sons and as many daughters, showed contempt for Latona, the mother of but two children, Apollo and Diana. In punishment for this,

Latona's children killed all the offspring of Niobe, and she herself was turned into a rock.

NYCTELIUS.— Y. G. 22.

A name of Bacchus; it was given to him because his orgies were celebrated at night. Serv. Æn. 4. 383.

OGYGES.— F. Q. 3. 8. 30. See Founders of Nations.

ŒNONE.— F. Q. 3. 9. 36; 6. 9. 36.

She was a river-nymph of Mt. Ida, whom Paris married while still a shepherd, and before he was acknowledged as the son of Priam. Together they lived a simple pastoral life, until their happiness was ended by the judgment which Paris made concerning the relative beauty of Juno, Minerva, and Venus, — a decision which gave Helen to Paris, and brought on the Trojan War.

The perfidy of Paris wounded Œnone, and Ovid embodies her protests in the form of a letter (*Her.* 5). See Apoll. 3. 12.6 for a statement of the simple facts.

It was said that Paris had a son, Corythus, by Œnone (Tzet. *Lyc.* 57), and Spenser skillfully calls him Parius, and makes him the progenitor of Paridell. See also **Apollo**.

OPS.— F. Q. 7. 7. 26.

Spenser mentions Ops as the goddess of the earth, a statement authorized by Macrobius, who says that Ops was regarded as the wife of Saturn, "quos, etiam nonnullis cælum ac terram esse persuasum est, Saturnumque a satu dictum, cuius causa de cælo est, et terram opem, cuius ope humanæ vitæ alimenta quæruntur, vel ab opere per quod fructus frugesque nascuntur." — *Sat.* 1. 10. 20.

ORCUS.— F. Q. 2. 12. 41; 6. 12. 26.

The ancients use this name to signify both the Infernal Regions and a god of Hell, synonymous with Pluto.

Spenser, in both these passages, speaks of Orcus as a grim, inexorable divinity. Compare *Il.* 9. 158, where he is described as so implacable that in the eyes of mortals he is the most hateful of the gods; and Horace, *Carm.* 2. 3, where he is said to be pitiless.

ORESTES.— F. Q. 4. 10. 27.

Among the celebrated friendships named in this passage, that of Pylades and Orestes is cited. The *Orestes* of Euripides brings out the strength and beauty of their devotion to each other in a conversation between the two friends, when Orestes is facing the wrath of the Argives over the murder of his mother. Orestes hails Pylades as the partner of his soul; and Pylades asks: —

>... Where shall friendship show its faith,
> If now in thy afflictions I forsake thee?

ORION.

>... And now in Ocean deep
> Orion, flying fast from hissing snake,
> His flaming head did hasten for to steep.
>
> *F. Q.* 2. 2. 46.

This poetical description of the setting of Orion rests upon the myth concerning his death. All authorities agree as to his life: it was that of a hunter devoted to the same pursuit that Diana loved; but there is not the same agreement as regards his death. Hyginus (*Fab.* 195) says simply that he was killed by Diana because of an attempt to violate her. Ovid (*Fast.* 5. 537) relates that, after Orion had boasted that there was no wild beast which he was unable to conquer, the earth sent forth a scorpion, which attempted to seize upon Latona. Orion, opposing it, was killed, and Latona added him to the number of the stars. According to Homer (*Od.* 5. 121) Aurora incurred the anger of Diana by her love for Orion, and in vengeance Diana pierced him with her arrows. Apollodorus (1. 4. 5) says that he was killed by the darts of Diana, either for challenging her to a game of discus, or for violating Opis. It will be seen that with no one of these accounts does Spenser exactly agree. He says: —

> Upon a dreadful scorpion he did ride,
> The same which by Dianaes doom unjust
> Slew great Orion.
>
> *F. Q.* 7. 7. 39.

For such an account of his death we must turn to Lucan 9. 836. See also Serv. *Æn.* 1. 539.

Hyginus (*Poet. Astron.* 2. Scorpius) says that the scorpion in the heavens is the one which the earth produced in defiance of

Orion's boast, and that Jupiter admitted it to the number of the stars that it might ever serve as a warning to men against too great self-confidence. He further adds that Diana obtained from Jupiter the favor that when the scorpion rose Orion should set.

In *F. Q.* 1. 3. 31 we have a reference to fierce Orion's hound. This is the dog-star, which Hyginus says (*Poet. Astron.* 2. Canis) was according to some accounts the dog of the hunter Orion.

For *F. Q.* 4. 11. 13, see **Sea-Gods**.

ORPHEUS.

What has already been said of Linus, who is mentioned as a poet in connection with Orpheus (*R. T.* 333), will apply to Orpheus, only that, in the group of half-historical and half-mythological characters to which they both belong, Orpheus, the reputed inventor of music, is the more important. Many are the works attributed to him, some of which are genuine and some spurious.

Among the scant earlier traditions respecting Orpheus, is that which represents the wonderful power of his music over men, beasts, and inanimate nature. Spenser refers to this in *F. Q.* 4. 2. 1; *R. T.* 607; *V. G.* 23; *Am.* 44. For the special reference to his allaying the discord among the followers of Jason, see **Argonautic Expedition**. Numerous passages, from the time of the lyric poets of Greece down to a much later day, might be quoted to support the general references; but perhaps no one better shows that his music had charms than *Met.* 10. 86 ff., where trees and beasts and birds are described as flocking about the tuneful bard, when, in his retirement among the mountains, he mourns the loss of his wife.

But the power of his lyre was not confined to the upper world; with it Orpheus dared to invade the realms of Hades in order to recover his beloved Eurydice to life, and by its spell the Stygian powers were appeased. This incident is enlarged upon in *V. G.* 55 ff., with which passage should be compared the more detailed and poetical accounts in *Georg.* 4. 454 ff. and *Met.* 10. 797 ff. See also *F. Q.* 4. 10. 58; *H. L.* 234; *Ep.* 16; and *R. T.* 391, where Spenser says that the temporary recovery of Eurydice was by favor of the Muses. This is most appropriate, for the ancients believed Orpheus to have been the child of Calliope, and the special care of Apollo and the Muses (Hyg. *Poet. Astron.* 2. Lyra).

ORSILOCHUS.—F. Q. 3. 4. 2. See Camilla.

ORTHRUS.—F. Q. 5. 10. 10. See Geryon.

OSIRIS.—F. Q. 5. 7. 2. See Isis.

OTHUS.—V. G. 47. See Ephialtes.

PÆON.—F. Q. 3. 4. 41. See Apollo.

PALEMON.—F. Q. 4. 11. 13. See Sea-Gods.

PALES.—V. G. 4; 15.

A Roman divinity of shepherds. Compare *Fast.* 4. 721 ff.

PALLAS.—Mui. 262 ff. See Arachne.

PALICI.

> Nor since that faire Calliope did lose
> Her loved Twinnes, the dearlings of her joy,
> Her Palici, whom her unkindly foes,
> The fatall Sisters, did for spight destroy,
> Whom all the Muses did bewaile long space,
> Was ever heard such wayling in this place.
>
> *T. M.* 15 ff.

An examination of ancient authorities reveals the fact that Spenser has erred in the mythology of this passage. The Palici were indeed twins, but the sons of Zeus and Thalia — not, however, the Muse Thalia, but a nymph, the daughter of Hephæstus — a presumable confusion, which resulted in the further confusion of the Muse Calliope with Thalia.

In the *Saturnalia* of Macrobius (5. 19. 16 ff.), there is a lengthy discussion of the Palici, from which it appears that Thalia, out of fear of the anger of Juno, implored the earth to swallow her. Her request was granted, and in due time there issued from the earth the twin sons of Zeus and Thalia. They were called Palici, "ἀπὸ τοῦ πάλιν ἱκέσθαι, *quoniam prius in terra immersi denuo inde reversi sunt.*" They were worshiped in Sicily.

PAN.—F. Q. 2. 9. 40. S. C. Jan. 17; Apr. 51; May 54, 111; June 30, 68; Nov. 8; Dec. 7, 46.

Since Pan was the god of sheep and shepherds, we should naturally expect to find his name often mentioned on the pages of a pastoral poem like the *Shepheard's Calender*. It is the case with the *Eclogues* of Virgil and also the *Idyls* of Theocritus, after which the *Shepheard's Calender* was avowedly patterned.

Sometimes Spenser used the name for that of Christ: thus E. K. says in one of his notes: "Great Pan is Christ, the very God of all shepherds, which calleth himself the 'greate, and good shepherd.' The name is most rightly (methinks) applyed to him; for Pan signifieth all, or omnipotent, which is only the Lord Jesus."

There are several references to Pan's sporting in song and dance with the nymphs, which are thoroughly consistent with the characterization of this rollicking god in the *Hom. Hymn to Pan*.

In *S. C.* Jan. 17, Colin Clout thus invokes Pan:—

And, Pan, thou shepheards God, that once didst love,
Pitie the paines that thou thyselfe didst prove.

This is a reference to Pan's unavailing love for Syrinx, mentioned also in Apr. 51. Ovid (*Met.* 1. 689 ff.) says that Syrinx was a Naiad who had devoted her virginity to Diana. When Pan became enamored of her, she fled from him to the river Ladon, in Arcadia, and besought help from the nymphs of that stream. They met her entreaties with the desired metamorphosis, and Syrinx was changed into reeds. And here the origin of the shepherd's flute, or syrinx, is poetically accounted for: Pan seized what he supposed to be his beloved Syrinx, but what proved to be only reeds of the marsh. As he held them in despair, the wind sighed among them, as if it too were lamenting the unrequited love of the god. Immediately Pan was charmed by the sound, and vowed that henceforth that should be his mode of communicating with the vanished nymph.

It is said that Pan became so elated with the music of this pipe that he dared challenge even Phœbus to a contest, a myth already referred to under **Apollo**.

F. Q. 2. 9. 40 contains a reference to a myth which is usually only hinted at in an obscure way in the classics: according to Schol. Theoc. *Idyl* 2. 17, Echo bore to Pan a daughter named Iynx, who, for trying to practice her love-charms upon Jove, was changed by Juno into the wry-neck (Lat. *iynx*) — a bird used by the ancients in conjurations and love-charms (see Pind. *Pyth.* 4. 380).

It is evident, however, that it is not the wry-neck, but more probably the cuckoo, that Spenser has in mind here; and it will be noticed also that our poet makes Pan, rather than Juno, responsible for the metamorphosis.

PANDIONIAN (maids). — V. G. 51. See Itys.

PANDORA. — T. M. 578; B. R. 19.; Am. 24.

When Spenser, after the manner of the Elizabethans, would offer his tribute of flattery to his sovereign, he calls her "the true Pandora of all heavenly graces," having in mind the meaning of the name — *the all-gifted one*.

When Jove wished to destroy the peace of man, says Hesiod (*Theog.* 571 ff.; *W. and D.* 60 ff.), he ordered Vulcan to make Pandora the type of all the fair sex. Endowed by the immortals with various charms, she allures man only to prove his bane: she is the drone, while man is the bee. It must have been this pessimistic wail of the old poet that Spenser had in mind when, in *Am.* 24, he says: —

> I thinke that I a new Pandora see
> Whom all the Gods in councell did agree
> Into this sinfull world from heaven to send;
> That she to wicked men a scourge should bee,
> For all their faults with which they did offend.

In *R. R.* 19 there is a reference to the famous box of Pandora. Hesiod says it contained all the ills to which flesh is heir, while other writers say it held only blessings; but when Pandora opened the box they escaped, thus, by their absence, proving to be ills. In the passage under consideration, the box which is likened to Pandora's contains both good and bad fortune.

PANOPE. — F. Q. 4. 11. 49. See Nereids.

In *F. Q.* 3. 8. 37 ff., the name is given to an aged nymph who keeps the house for Proteus at the bottom of the sea — seemingly an instance of Spenser's original mythology.

PARIS. — F. Q. 2. 7. 55; 3. 9. 34; 4. 11. 19; 6. 9. 36; V. G. 67. See Helen; Œnone; Achilles.

PASIPHAE. — F. Q. 3. 2. 41.

This reference to the passion of Pasiphae, the wife of Minos, and mother of the Minotaur, is explained by Apoll. 3. 1. 4. and Hyg. *Fab.* 40.

PASITHEA. — F. Q. 4. 11. 49. See **Nereids**.

PEGASUS. — F. Q. 3. 11. 42; R. T. 426 ff.

For the parentage of Pegasus, see **Medusa**.

> Then, who so will with vertuous deeds assay
> To mount to heaven, on Pegasus must ride,
> And with sweete Poets verse be glorifide.
> *R. T.* 426.

The idea which associates Pegasus with the Muses as patrons of poetry, which in our day is embodied in the expression "to mount Pegasus," arose from the myth concerning the fount of Hippocrene on Helicon, which, it was said, was produced by the striking of the hoof of Pegasus against the ground, when, on the occasion of the universal delight over the singing of the Muses, he was hidden by Poseidon to arrest the upward movement of Helicon. See Paus. 9. 31; Stat. *Theb.* 4. 60. For the reference to the winged steed in *R. T.* 646, see **Andromeda**.

PELEUS. — F. Q. 6. 10. 22; 7. 7. 12; V. G. 61 ff.

These passages all refer to the marriage of Peleus, the son of Æacus, and Thetis, the daughter of Nereus, in support of which see *Iliad, passim;* Apoll. 3. 13. 5; *Met.* 11. 217 ff.; Catullus, *Nupt. Pel. et Thet.* It should be noticed that, whereas Apollodorus says the marriage occurred on Mt. Pelion, Ovid says it was by the bay of Hæmonia — a name which, it is possible, Spenser had in mind when, in the second passage referred to, he says the nuptials were celebrated on Mt. Hæmus. As to the "spousall hymne," see **Apollo**.

PELIAS. — F. Q. 4. 11. 14. See **Sea-Gods**.

PENELOPE. — F. Q. 5. 7. 39; V. G. 54; Am. 23.

These references to Penelope, the classical type of constancy; to the web which she devised to put off her suitors; and to her final reunion with Ulysses, — are all taken from the *Odyssey, passim.*

PENTHESILEA. — F. Q. 3. 4. 2.

Spenser here says that Homer refers to the bold feats of Penthesilea; this, however, is not true, unless we take Homer in a very broad sense to include certain extensions of his works, like the writings of Quintus Calaber. This author has much to say of Penthesilea and her Amazons (1. 18 ff.).

For the death of Penthesilea, see **Amazons**.

PERSEPHONE. — T. M. 164; V. G. 53. See **Proserpina**.

PERSEUS. — R. T. 648. See Andromeda.

PHAETON. — F. Q. 5. 8. 40; V. G. 25.

The myth of Phaeton, whom his father **Phœbus**, in token of his paternity, allowed to drive the horses of the sun, is here cited. It is the subject of an extensive passage in the *Metamorphoses* (1. 748 ff.), to which Spenser was, no doubt, indebted. When, through the careless driving of Phaeton, the world seemed in danger of being consumed, Jupiter struck him with a thunderbolt; Phaeton, falling into the river Po, was henceforth mourned by his sisters, who were transformed to poplar-trees. Ovid, like Spenser, mentions the fright which the scorpion caused, but says it was Phaeton, not the horses, who was thus excited. See also *T. M.* 7.

PHAO. — F. Q. 3. 2. 20.

Not a character from classical mythology. See note on this passage in Child's edition of Spenser: "The story of this tower is apparently derived from some mediæval legend about the Pharos of Ptolemy Philadelphus, in which, perhaps, Phao took the place of the historical Arsinoe. The king was, no doubt, confounded with Ptolemy the Astronomer, who, says Warton, 'was famous among the Eastern writers and their followers for his skill in operations of glass.'"

PHAO. — F. Q. 4. 11. 49. See Nereids.

PHERUSA. — F. Q. 4. 11. 49. See Nereids.

PHILOMELA. — T. M. 236. See **Itys**.

PHLEGETHON.

A river bounding Tartarus, with waves of torrent fire (*Æn.* 6. 551). Compare *F. Q.* 1. 5. 33; 2. 6. 50; *V. G.* 56; 78.

According to *F. Q.* 4. 2. 1., Discord is appropriately described as a firebrand kindled in Phlegethon. Compare *F. Q.* 2. 5. 22.

For *F. Q.* 2. 4. 41, see **Erebus**.

PHŒAX. — F. Q. 4. 11. 15. See **Founders of Nations**.

PHŒBE. — F. Q. 1. 7. 5; 2. 2. 44; 3. 6. 24; 4. 5. 14; 7. 6. 21; S. C. Apr. 65; June 31; July 63; Dec. 84; Co. Cl. 342; Ep. 149. See **Diana**.

PHŒBUS. — F. Q. 1. Int. 4; 1. 1. 23; 1. 2. 1; 1. 2. 29; 1. 4. 9; 1. 5. 2; 1. 5. 20; 1. 5. 44; 1. 6. 6; 1. 7. 29; 1. 7. 34; 1. 11. 5; 1. 11. 31; 1. 12. 2; 2. 8. 5; 2. 9. 10; 2. 9. 48; 2. 10. 3; 2. 11. 19; 2. 12. 52; 3. 2. 24; 3. 3. 4; 3. 5. 27; 3. 6. 2; 3. 6. 44; 3. 6. 45; 3. 10. 1; 3. 10. 45; 3. 11. 36; 4. 6. 1; 4. 11. 52; 5. 3. 19; 5. 11. 62; 6. 3. 29; 7. 6. 35; 7. 6. 39; 7. 7. 12; 7. 7. 51; S. C. Jan. 73; Apr. 73; June 68; Aug. 83; Oct. 3. Nov. 14; T. M. 7; 330; V. G. 2; 7; 21; 78; 84; Mui. 79; V. W. Y. 2; Ep. 77; 121. See **Apollo**.

PHOENIX. — F. Q. 4. 11. 15. See **Founders of Nations**.

PHOLOE. — F. Q. 1. 6. 15.

Pholoe is here alluded to as a nymph beloved by Silvanus. The name belongs primarily to a mountain in Arcadia which was frequented by Pan (*Fast.* 2. 273), and, according to classic usage, might be transferred to an Oread, or nymph inhabiting the mountain. In making her the beloved of Silvanus, Spenser is only carrying out the frequent classical identifications of the rustic divinities, Silvanus and Pan.

PHORCYS. — F. Q. 4. 11. 13. See **Sea-Gods**.

PHRIXUS. — F. Q. 5. Int. 5. See **Helle**.

PHRYGIAN (mother). — R. R. 6. See **Cybele**.

PIRITHOUS. — F. Q. 4. 10. 27.

The friendship between Theseus and Pirithous was proverbial among the ancients. Thus Ovid speaks of it as "felix concordia" (*Met.* 8. 303).

PLUTO.

The Infernal Regions are referred to as the bower or house of Pluto in *F. Q.* 1. 5. 14; 1. 5. 32; 2. 7. 21; 2. 7. 24; 4. 3. 13; *S. C.* Oct. 29. Since he was the king of the Lower World, this designation is appropriate. Compare *Il.* 15. 188; *Æn.* 6, *passim*. *F. Q.* 2. 7. 21 ff., which describes the beings sitting before the realm of Pluto, is copied after *Æn.* 6. 273 ff.: "Just before the porch and in the opening of the jaws of Orcus, Grief and Avenging Pains have set their couch; and there ghastly Diseases dwell," etc.

Pluto is further mentioned as the husband of Proserpina in *F. Q.* 1. 1. 37; 1. 4. 11, for which see **Proserpina**; also as the master of Cerberus in *F. Q.* 6. 12. 35, for which see **Cerberus**.

PODALIRIUS.—F. Q. 6. 6. 1.

Homer (*Il.* 2. 732) says that Podalirius and Machaon were two excellent physicians, sons of Æsculapius. Ovid (*A. A.* 2. 735) says: "As great as was Podalirius among the Greeks in the art of healing, ... so great a lover am I."

POLYNOME.—F. Q. 4. 11. 50. See **Nereids**.

PONTOPOREA.—F. Q. 4. 11. 50. See **Nereids**.

PORIS.—F. Q. 4. 11. 49. See **Nereids**.

PROCRUSTES.—F. Q. 7. 6. 29.

This reference to Procrustes as among those who had been too presumptuous in their aspirations, and, thus offending Jupiter, were punished by him, is not at all to the point. Procrustes was a robber of Attica, who waylaid strangers and stretched them upon a bed; if they were too long or too short, he adjusted matters by cutting off or stretching out their limbs. This monster met his fate at the hands of Theseus, and is, therefore, merely an example of a criminal deservedly punished; and so, as said above, the circumstances of his life and death do not warrant Spenser in introducing him in this particular connection. See Diod. Sic. 4. 59. 5; Hyg. *Fab.* 38.

PRIAM.

Since Priam was the king of the Trojans, Troy is appropriately called Priam's city, realm, or town in *F. Q.* 2. 9. 48 3. 9.

36; 3. 9. 38; 4. 11. 19.   Compare *Il.* 1. 19; 22. 251; *Æn.* 2. 191.
For *F. Q.* 2. 3. 31, see **Amazons.**

PROMETHEUS. — F. Q. 2. 10. 70; 7. 6. 29.

Spenser says that Prometheus created man from the organs of beasts, that he stole fire from the gods to animate this creation, and that he was, for this audacity, deprived by Jove of life (that is, its freedom).

This account accords with the later rather than the earlier classics. Thus Hesiod (*Theog.* 535 ff.) says that Prometheus tried to practice deception upon Jove in the division of a sacrificial animal, and that Jove, in his anger, denied fire to men. Prometheus, however, secretly stole some sparks from the gods, and, concealing them in a hollow tube, brought them to the earth for the use of man. This so enraged Jupiter that he sent Pandora as a scourge to men, had Prometheus chained to a pillar, and sent an eagle every day to feed upon his never-dying liver; until, after the lapse of years, the hapless Prometheus was released by Hercules.

The *Prometheus* of Æschylus, also, while not agreeing with the account of Hesiod, does not more nearly accord with this passage from Spenser. Neither knows aught of Prometheus as the creator of man, nor of his stealing fire to animate this creation, although both support Spenser in the matter of the punishment of Prometheus.

It is to Latin authorities of a later period that our poet is indebted for these points: thus Ovid (*Met.* 1. 76 ff.) says that Prometheus made man of earth and water, but says nothing of his creating him from the organs of animals and animating him with fire. Horace, on the other hand, authorizes the first of these statements: —

> Fertur Prometheus addere principi
> Limo coactus particulam undique
> Desectam, et insani leonis
> Vim stomacho adposuisse nostro.
>
> *Carm.* 1. 16.

and Fulgentius, in his treatment of the myth of Prometheus, adds that the creator of man stole fire from the celestial regions to animate his work.

PRONÆA. — F. Q. 4. 11. 50. See **Nereids**.

PROSERPINA. — F. Q. 1. 2. 2; 1. 4. 11; 2. 7. 53; 3. 11. 1; R. T. 373; T. M. 164; V. G. 53.

All these passages refer to Proserpina in the capacity of Queen of Hell, after she was captured by Pluto, and borne as his bride from the Upper to the Lower World. For the details of her abduction, see the *Hom. Hymn to Ceres*, and Claudian, *De Raptu Proserpinæ*. See also *Od.* 11, *passim*; *Æn.* 6. 397, where she is referred to as the queen of the grim Pluto.

Spenser's description of the Garden of Proserpina in *F. Q.* 2. 7. 51 ff. is a finely imagined amplification of certain suggestions in the classics; thus, in *Odyssey* 10. 508 ff., there is mentioned a grove of Proserpina, at the utmost western limit of the Ocean. It consists of poplar and willow trees, and forms the entrance to Hell. In Claudian's *De Raptu Proserpinæ* 290 ff., Pluto describes to his bride, among other delights awaiting her in Hades, a grove which is to be sacred to her : —

> Est etiam lucis arbor prædives opacis,
> Fulgentes viridi ramos curvata metallo.
> Hæc tibi sacra datur, fortunatumque tenebis
> Autumnum, et fulvis semper ditabere pomis.

This last passage in particular probably suggested to Spenser the tree laden with the golden apples, or perhaps it was *Æn.* 6. 136 ff., — lines which describe the tree with the bough of gold which was sacred to Proserpina.

PROTEUS. — F. Q. 1. 2. 10; 3. 4. 25 ff.; 3. 8. 29 ff.; 4. 11. 2 ff.; 4. 12. 3 ff.; Co. Cl. 248.

From these passages we learn that Proteus was the shepherd of the seas, who attended the flocks of Neptune; that he could change his form at will; that he was inspired with the gift of prophecy; and that he lived in a huge cave, walled about by the waves of the sea. His personal appearance is thus described : —

> An aged sire with head all frory hore,
> And sprinckled frost upon his deawy beard.

All this is thoroughly consistent with that passage in the *Odyssey* (4. 384 ff.) which describes the prophetic interview which

Proteus granted Telemachus, but only after trying to evade it by changing himself into a lion, a pard, a boar, a dragon, a stream, and a tree. See also *Georg.* 4. 388 ff. — a passage patterned after that of the *Odyssey.*

PROTO.—F. Q. 4. 11. 48. See Nereids.

PROTOMEDÆA.—F. Q. 4. 11. 49. See Nereids.

PSAMATHE.—F. Q. 4. 11. 51. See Nereids.

PSYCHE.—F. Q. 3. 6. 50; Mui. 131.

Both these passages refer to the story of **Cupid and Psyche** as related in the fourth book of the *Metamorphoses* of Apuleius. Psyche was a mortal, who, by her surpassing beauty, excited the jealousy of Venus. The goddess commanded her son Cupid to curse Psyche with a love for the most wretched of mortals. Cupid himself, however, fell a victim to the charms of the hapless Psyche, and visited her every night, taking his flight before daybreak, that she might not know who her lover was. This state of bliss would have been enduring had not Psyche violated the injunction of Cupid, and sought to discover his identity. Bending over him with a lamp, she let fall a drop of oil upon his shoulder; he awoke, and in anger vanished from her sight. Here the troubles of Psyche began: in the search for her lost love, she fell into the hands of Venus, who subjected her to various hardships. But her wretchedness had an end; for Cupid made an appeal to Jupiter, who summoned the gods to an assembly, and in presence of them all he united the lovers in wedlock. Moreover, in order that they might be of equal rank, Jupiter extended to Psyche a cup of ambrosia, and bade her quaff it, with these words: "Take this, Psyche, and be immortal; nor shall Cupid ever depart from your embrace, but these nuptials of yours shall be perpetual."

Thus Psyche, the soul, after enduring the purification that hardship and suffering bring, was elevated to heaven, and joined to Love in everlasting union.

In due time, the story relates, a daughter was born to them who was called Pleasure. Compare *H. L.* 288.

PYLADES.—F. Q. 4. 10. 27. See Orestes.

PYLIAN (sire).— F. Q. 2. 9. 48.

This is Nestor, whose native city was Pylos. His reputation for sage counsel and remarkable age is due principally to the *Iliad* and the *Odyssey*; for he took an active part in the Trojan War, not only as a warrior at the head of his Pylian forces, but as a wise counselor whose advice was often sought by the Greeks. It was a common tradition that he survived three generations of men. Thus Homer (*Il.* 1. 250 ff.) says, "Two generations of mortal men already had he seen perish, that had been of old time born and nurtured with him in goodly Pylos, and he was king among the third."

PYRACMON.— F. Q. 4. 5. 37. See Brontes.

PYRRHA.— F. Q. 5. Int. 2. See Deucalion.

PYTHIAS.— F. Q. 4. 10. 27.

Diodorus Siculus (21. 10. 4) tells the well-known story of the friendship between Damon and Pythias (Phintias). When Pythias had been condemned to death for his share in a plot against Dionysius, the tyrant of Syracuse, he asked for a respite of a few days that he might arrange his business affairs, promising to secure a friend who would serve as pledge, and who, if he himself did not return by a certain time, would die in his stead. Such a friend was found in Damon, who, however, was saved from the fulfillment of his promise by the opportune arrival of Pythias. As might be expected, Dionysius was so filled with admiration at this unusual devotion that he pardoned Pythias, and asked that he himself might share in such a friendship.

RHÆSUS.— See Rhesus.

RHESUS.— V. G. 67.

The fall of Strymonian Rhesus at the hands of Ulysses and Diomedes is related in *Il.* 10, in close connection with the violent death of Dolon. Rhesus was a king of Thrace who sided with the Trojans. While he and his men were asleep, Ulysses and Diomedes murdered them, and carried away their famous white horses.

The epithet **Strymonian** is explained by the fact that later writers regarded Rhesus as the son of Strymon, a river of Thrace.

SAO.—F. Q. 4. 11. 48. See **Nereids**.

SATURN.

In *F. Q.* 7. 6. 27 Spenser says that Saturn was the son of Uranus, thus following Hesiod (*Theog.* 137), Saturn being the Greek Cronus, with whom he was identified by the Romans. Then our poet proceeds to relate the circumstances by which Saturn and his descendants won the throne from Titan, an elder son of Uranus. For this unusual recital of the affair, see **Titan**.

Saturn is mentioned as the father of Jove in *F. Q.* 7. 6. 2. See **Jove**.

In *F. Q.* 3. 11. 43 Saturn is called the lover of Erigone, for whom he transformed himself into a Centaur, and in *F. Q.* 7. 7. 40 he is mentioned as the father of Chiron by Nais. For a discussion of these passages, see **Erigone** and **Nais**.

The reign of Saturn, "the golden age," when peace and plenty abounded (*F. Q.* 5. Int. 9; *M. H. T.* 151), is explained by Ovid (*Fast.* 1. 233 ff.) and Macrobius (*Sat.* 1. 7 ff.).

When Saturn was expelled from heaven by Jove, he took up his abode in Latium, where he was hospitably received by Janus. He taught the aborigines the uses of agriculture, and a reign of universal prosperity ensued. In *Met.* 1. 89 ff., we have a detailed description of this golden age, which Spenser has paraphrased in *F. Q.* 5. Int. 9.

The planet of Saturn is mentioned in *F. Q.* 2. 9. 52; 5. Int. 8; 7. 7. 52. Its baneful influence over human life is hinted at in the adjectives "oblique" and "grim," while the adjective "old" has reference to the belief that Saturn was the first of the gods. It is common to find in ancient literature references to the malign influence of Saturn, as for instance in Horace *Carm.* 2. 17. The reason for this belief is discussed at some length by Macrobius *Com.* 19. 20 — a subject that is within the province of astrology rather than that of mythology.

SCYLLA.—V. G. 68.

With this compare *Odyssey* 12. 73 ff., and *Æn.* 3. 420 ff., whence it appears that Scylla was a monster inhabiting a certain dangerous rock between Italy and Sicily. Her voice was dreadful to hear, and her form frightful to look upon. Surrounded by her sea-dogs, she stood ready to devour all ships that came her way.

SEA-GODS. — F. Q. 4. 11. 12.

Although the direct source of this catalogue of names is probably the *Mythology* of Natalis Comes, yet there are ultimate authorities in the classics which justify the statement that these divinities were the offspring of Neptune; provided that too strict an interpretation is not put upon *Neptune*, and that the name be understood to stand for Pontus and Oceanus also. When, however, our poet says that Amphitrite is the mother of these gods, he does so on his own authority, unsupported by the classics. For the descriptive words and phrases accompanying the names, Spenser is for the most part indebted to the ancients.

Phorcys,

> The father of that fatall brood,
> By whom those old Heroes wonne such fame.

Son of Pontus, and father of the Gorgons (Apoll. 1. 2. 6).

Glaucus, "that wise soothsayer understood." According to *Met.* 13. 904 ff., he was originally a mortal. Having placed some fishes on the grass, he noticed that they ate of it, and with renewed life jumped again into the water. Thereupon Glaucus himself partook of the grass, and in a frenzy leaped into the sea, where he became a god.

His remarkable prophetic power is alluded to by Apollonius Rhodius (1. 1310).

Palæmon,

> And tragicke Inoes sonne, the which became
> A God of seas through his mad mothers blame,
> Now hight Palemon, and is saylers frend.

This is explained by Apoll. 3. 4. 3 and *Met.* 4. 416 ff. The jealousy of Juno had been excited against Ino, the wife of Athamas, and aunt of Bacchus, and she caused Ino and her husband to become mad. The results of their frenzy were most distressing; for Athamas, after killing his eldest son, pursued Ino, who bore in her arms the infant Melicertes, to the brink of the sea, where the maddened Ino plunged with her child beneath the waves.

At this point Neptune changed them to sea-gods, altering the name of Melicertes to Palæmon, who was supposed to bring aid to the storm-tossed sailor.

The following table, also deduced from Apollodorus, shows that Palæmon was a descendent of Neptune: —

>NEPTUNE
>|
>AGENOR
>|
>CADMUS
>|
>INO
>|
>PALÆMON

Brontes, "great." He was one of the Cyclops, mentioned by Hesiod (*Theog.* 140), who, according to him, were the sons of Uranus and Gæa. They are, however, mentioned by other writers as the sons of Poseidon (see *Od.* 9. 412).

Astræus,

>. . . that did shame
>Himselfe with incest of his kin unkend.

Plut. *De Fluv.* 21. 1 calls him a son of Poseidon, and mentions the fact of his incest.

Orion,

>And huge Orion, that doth tempest still portend.

Orion was, according to Apoll. 1. 4. 3, the son of Neptune; and his great size is also mentioned there. After his death he was placed in the heavens as a constellation, whose rising was generally supposed to be accompanied by storms. Thus, in *Æn.* 1. 535, Orion is called *stormy*. See **Orion**.

Cteatus, "the rich Cteatus." Apoll. 2. 7. 2 names him and his brother Eurytus as the sons of Neptune, and says that they surpassed all their contemporaries in power (δυνάμει). The Greek word may mean *wealth* as well as *bodily strength;* thus, in the Latin translation of this passage by Benedictus Ægius Spolatinus, the single Greek word is translated by "viribus atque opibus," and on similar grounds Spenser uses the epithet "rich."

Eurytus, "long." See above. But why he is called *long* is not evident.

Neleus and Pelias, "lovely brethren both." They were,

according to Apoll. 1. 9. 8, the twin sons of Neptune by Tyro. The adjective *lovely* seems to be inserted by Spenser without any special authority from the classics.

Chrysaor, "mightie." According to Apoll. 2. 4. 3, he was the son of Neptune, who, with Pegasus, sprang from the blood of Medusa, and also the father of the monster Geryon. Hesiod (*Theog.* 281) speaks of Chrysaor as great.

Caicus, "strong." He is mentioned in *Theog.* 343 among the rivers who were the offspring of Ocean and Tethys. He is called strong because the Caicus drains a large plain in Mysia (Strab. 13. 1. 68).

Eurypulus, "that calmes the waters wroth." He is mentioned in Apoll. 2. 7. 1 as a son of Neptune. The particular power ascribed to him seems to have no parallel in the classics.

Euphœmus,

> . . . that upon them [the waters] goth,
> As, on the ground, without dismay or dread.

He is mentioned in Apoll. 1. 9. 16 as a son of Neptune.

The allusion to his fearlessness in walking upon the sea is explained by Hyg. *Fab.* 14: "Hic super aquas sicco pede cucurrisse dicitur."

Eryx, "Fierce Eryx." He is mentioned in Apoll. 2. 5. 10 as a son of Neptune who ruled in a part of Sicily, and who fought with Hercules; hence "fierce."

Alebius, "that know'th the waters depth and doth their bottome tread." Alebius is the Alebion of Apoll. 2. 5. 10. He was a son of Neptune, who attacked Hercules as he was passing through Liguria with the oxen of Geryon.

The description seems to be fanciful on Spenser's part.

Asopus, "And sad Asopus, comely with his hoarie head." He was, according to Apoll. 3. 12. 6, a son of Oceanus and the father of Ægina, whom Jupiter carried away; hence the epithet *sad.* Since he was the father of numerous sons and daughters, Spenser very appropriately represents him with a hoary head.

SEMELE.—F. Q. 3. 11. 33.

The tragic death of **Semele,** caused by beholding Jove in all his glory, is related in *Met.* 3. 253 ff. Juno, stung with jealousy at Jove's intrigue with Semele, visited her in the guise of her nurse, and suggested to Semele that she request Jupiter to confirm his godship by appearing to her in all his majesty. Juno knew that no mortal eye could behold such glory with impunity, but the unsuspecting Semele followed the advice given her. Jupiter swore to grant any request she might make; thus it was too late to retract when Semele asked that she might behold him in the majesty with which he was accustomed to appear to Juno. "The mortal body of Semele," says Ovid, "could not endure the ethereal shock, and she was killed amid her nuptial presents."

SEMIRAMIS.— F. Q. 1. 5. 50; 2. 10. 56.

The account which Diodorus Siculus gives of the death of Semiramis does not accord with that given in the first of these passages; but it is probable that his story at this point is only an abridgment of that of Ctesias, whom he follows in his narration of Assyrian history. Justin (1. 1), however, who also is indebted to Ctesias for his information, says that Semiramis was killed by her son on account of her unlawful love for him. See Ninus.

SILVANUS.— F. Q. 1. 6. 7; 1. 6. 33.

A very striking passage is that in which Silvanus, a rustic deity, with his fauns and satyrs, his hamadryads and naiads, are represented as overcome with admiration at the loveliness of Una, who had been led into their woody retreat. Silvanus is pictured as an old man, leaning on a cypress staff, his waist twined with ivy. It is true that the ancients represent him as advanced in years (see *Georg.* 2. 494), but not as feeble: thus Ovid says he was "suis semper juvenilior annis" (*Met.* 14. 639). The cypress staff was, no doubt, suggested to Spenser by *Georg.* 1. 20, where Silvanus is said to be carrying a young cypress-tree, or by the myth which relates the love of the god for Cyparissus, to which Spenser refers later on. See Cyparissus.

When the Satyrs come bringing Una, "that flowre of fayth and beautie excellent," to Silvanus, the beauty of his Dryope pales in his estimation, and Pholoe seems no longer fair. See Dryope and Pholoe.

SISYPHUS. — F. Q. 1. 5. 35.

Among those who, in the Lower World, were suffering the penalty of crimes committed in this, was Sisyphus: —

> And Sisyphus an huge round stone did reele
> Against an hill, ne might from labour lin.

This is consistent with *Od.* 11. 593; *Met.* 4. 460; 10. 44: that is, Ulysses, Juno, and Orpheus, when they visited the Lower World, all saw Sisyphus at his futile task of rolling a huge stone up a hill; when the stone reached the top, down it fell, and the labor must be renewed. While there is general agreement among the ancients as to the manner of his punishment, various crimes are mentioned as the cause of it.

SPIO. — F. Q. 4. 11. 48. See **Nereids**.

STHENOBŒA. — F. Q. 1. 5. 50.

The suicide of Sthenobœa, the wife of Prœtus, is related by Hyginus (*Fab.* 57). She fell in love with Bellerophon; but her affection was repulsed, and she killed herself in despair. Hyginus, however, does not mention the means by which she committed suicide, and other writers say she took poison; therefore Spenser is original in saying she did it by choking herself with a rope.

STYGIAN. — See **Styx**.

STYX.

A river of the Infernal Regions, mentioned in *Æn.* 6, *passim*. Hence Spenser speaks of the bitter wave of hellish Styx (*F. Q.* 2. 8. 20); of the black Stygian lake (*F. Q.* 1. 5. 10; 5. 11. 32); and of the black shadow of the Stygian shore (*V. G.* 48).

The references to ghosts wandering upon the banks of the Styx (*F. Q.* 1. 4. 48; 3. 2. 52; 3. 7. 14) are to be explained in the light of *Æn.* 6. 325 ff.: "All this crowd that you behold is forlorn and unburied. . . . And he [Charon] is not allowed to convey them between the dreadful banks, and across the roaring stream, before their bones have been laid in their place of rest. A hundred years they roam, and flit about these coasts; then at last they are received, and visit again the pool they long to win."

With *F. Q.* 3. 6. 24, which refers to a vow by the Stygian lake, "whose sad annoy The Gods doe dread," compare *Æn.* 6. 324: "the Stygian lake, by whose divinity the gods dread to swear and violate [their oath]."

With *R. R.* 15 compare *Æn.* 6. 439: "and Styx, nine times rolling between, confines them."

In *F. Q.* 2. 5. 22, Spenser seems to have confused the river Styx with Phlegethon; since it is that river, and not the Styx, which, according to *Æn.* 6. 550, rolls along torrents of flame.

Since the Styx is the most important of the rivers of the Lower World, Spenser very appropriately speaks of the Lower World itself as the Stygian realms, *F. Q.* 2. 12. 41 (see **Mercury**); of the Stygian gods, *F. Q.* 3. 6. 46 (see **Adonis**) and *F. Q.* 4. 3. 32; of the Stygian Prince, *F. Q.* 4. 10. 58 (see **Eurydice**); of the Stygian powers, *V. G.* 55; of the Stygian strands, *Daph.* 20.

In *F. Q.* 4. 11. 4 the Styx is personified as the Grandame of the Gods, with which passage compare Hyginus (*Fab.* Pref.), where Styx is said to be the offspring of Night and Erebus, who were of the first generation after Chaos. See **Erebus**.

For *F. Q.* 1. 1. 37, a passage in which the Styx and Cocytus are represented as quaking at the name of Gorgon, see **Gorgon**.

SYRINX.—S. C. Apr. 50, 93. See **Pan**.

SYLVANUS.—F. Q. 1. 6. 7; 1. 6. 33. See **Silvanus**.

TALUS.—F. Q. 5. 1. 11.

This man of iron mold, who, with an iron flail, separated truth from falsehood, is the same whom (pseudo-) Plato (*Minos* 320 C) describes as the guardian of the laws of Crete, which he had written upon brazen tables. Apollodorus, however, assures us that he was made of brass (1. 9. 26).

TANTALUS.

The description of the punishment of Tantalus in *F. Q.* 2. 7. 58 ff. is a copy of the similar passage in *Od.* 11. 582 ff. Tantalus is mentioned also among those accursed ones whom Juno and Orpheus saw in the Lower World (*Met.* 4. 458; 10. 41). See also *F. Q.* 1. 5. 35; *H. L.* 200.

The reason for the particular kind of punishment inflicted upon Tantalus is hinted at in the lines:—

> Lo! Tantalus, I here tormented lye:
> Of whom high Jove wont whylome feasted bee;
> Lo! here I now for want of food doe dye.

From an examination of the ancients, it seems probable that the second line of this passage should read, "Who of high Jove wont whylome feasted bee;" for that Tantalus was accustomed to eat at the table of the gods is vouched for by the ancients, where there is but one occasion on record where the gods feasted with him. It is said that Jove was accustomed to confide in Tantalus when he dined with him, and that Tantalus revealed the secrets of the immortals to men, for which he was thus punished in Hades. See Hyg. *Fab.* 82; 83; *Met.* 6. 173.

That Agamemnon was of the stock of **Tantalus**, as stated in *V. G.* 69, is seen from the following table:—

TANTALUS
|
PELOPS
|
ATREUS
|
AGAMEMNON

TARTARUS.—F. Q. 1. 7. 44; 2. 12. 6; V. G. 56; 68; M. H. T. 1294.

Compare *Æn.* 6. 577 ff., where Tartarus is described as that portion of the Lower World devoted to the punishment of the wicked.

TELAMON.—V. G. 61; 65.

For the parentage of Telamon, see **Æacus**. For the marriage of Telamon with Ixione, see **Hesione**.

The son of Telamon referred to in the second passage is Ajax, for an account of whose valor see **Æacides**.

TETHYS.

> Next came the aged Ocean and his Dame
> Old Tethys, th' oldest two of all the rest;
> For all the rest of those two parents came,
> Which afterward both sea and land possest.
>
> *F. Q.* 4. 11. 18.

According to the *Theogony* of Hesiod, Ocean and Tethys were ancient indeed, for they were the children of Heaven and

Earth. From their union sprang numerous rivers and Oceanides; so that Spenser is somewhat justified in the sweeping statement which he makes regarding the offspring of Ocean and Tethys.

The name Tethys is sometimes used by the ancients for the sea itself, as in *Met.* 2. 69, with which compare *F. Q.* 1. 1. 39; 1. 3. 31; 2. 12. 26; *R. R.* 20.

THALIA.—F. Q. 4. 11. 49. See **Nereids**.

THALIA.—F. Q. 6. 10. 22. See **Graces**.

THAUMANTES.—F. Q. 5. 3. 25. See **Thaumas**.

THAUMAS.—F. Q. 5. 3. 25.

Iris is here referred to as the daughter of Thaumantes. It should be Thaumas, who was, according to *Met.* 11. 647, the father of Iris.

THEMIS.—F. Q. 5. 9. 31. See **Litæ**.

THEMISTE.—F. Q. 4. 11. 51. See **Nereids**.

THESEUS.

For Theseus as husband of Ariadne (*F. Q.* 6. 10. 13), see **Ariadne**; as the father of a cursed son (*F. Q.* 5. 8. 43), see **Hippolytus**; as 'feare' [mate] of Pirithous (*F. Q.* 4. 10. 27), see **Pirithous**.

> Theseus condemned to endless slouth by law.
> *F. Q.* 1. 5. 35.

This seems to be a paraphrase of *Æn.* 6. 617: "Unhappy Theseus sits and will sit there forever." Theseus had assisted Pirithous in his attempt to carry away Proserpina from the realm of Pluto, for which they were both cast into chains; but it is usually related that the punishment of Theseus lasted only until he was released by Hercules. See Diod. Sic. 4. 63. 4.

THETIS.

As the wife of Peleus, Thetis is mentioned in *F. Q.* 6. 10. 22; *F. Q.* 7. 7. 12; *V. G.* 62, for which see **Peleus**.

> For not to have been dipt in Lethe lake,
> Could save the sonne of Thetis from to die;
> But that blinde bard did him immortall make
> With verses, dipt in deaw of Castalie.
> *R. T.* 429 ff.

Since Achilles is the central figure of the *Iliad*, our poet may well say that Homer made him immortal. The tradition, however, that Thetis dipped her son in the Styx (Spenser says *Lethe lake*) to make him immortal is, notwithstanding E. K.'s note on S. C. March 97, of later date than Homer. See Stat. *Achilles* 1. 269; Fulgentius, *De Peleo et Thetide*.

As one of the Nereids, Thetis is mentioned in F. Q. 4. 11. 48. See **Nereids**.

The name is employed by metonymy for the sea in R. R. 4, just as Neptune and Tethys are used elsewhere. For this post-Augustan use of the term, see Mart. 10. 30.

THRACIAN (maid).— F. Q. 3. 11. 35.

A comparison of this reference with its evident source, *Met.* 6. 114, shows that the Thracian maid is Deois; that is, Proserpina, daughter of Deo, or Ceres. The adjective Thracian, as applied to Proserpina, is explained from the fact that Cotys, or Cotytto, a divinity sometimes identified with Proserpina, was worshiped in Thrace. See Strab. 10. 3. 16.

TINDARID (lass).— F. Q. 4. 11. 19. See Helen.

TISIPHONE.— V. G. 43.

Compare *Æn.* 6. 555 ff., where Tisiphone is described as a Fury, guarding the vestibule of Tartarus. She is clothed in a bloody robe, and is further described in these words: "Tisiphone, the avenger, armed with her whip, unceasingly lashes the shuddering criminals, and taunts them withal, and with her left hand brandishing her grim serpents, summons her ruthless sisterhood."

TITAN.

The story to which reference is made in F. Q. 7. 6. 27 is told by Natalis Comes, and is not the usual familiar account of the way by which Saturn obtained the throne of heaven. (See Jove.) According to Natalis Comes, Titan was the elder brother of Saturn, who was persuaded to abdicate the throne on condition that Saturn would kill all children who might be born to him. This was in order that Saturn might have no descendants to succeed him. The compact was agreed upon, and Saturn devoured one child after another. Jove, however, escaped the fate of his brothers and sisters; hence Spenser's reference to the "Corybantes slight," which is explained under **Cybele**.

This myth, it will be seen, is better adapted to enforce the claims of Mutability than the usual one would be, and hence it was seized upon by our poet.

In the second stanza of this same canto, reference is made to the familiar story of Jove's overthrow of Saturn and his brother Titans (see **Jove**); and the statement is made that many of the descendants of the Titans survived, among whom Hecate and Bellona are especially mentioned. It is very true that the name of Titan is applied in the classics to various divinities — among them Themis, Phœbe, and even Hecate (see Serv. Æn. 4. 511) — but it would be difficult to say on what authority Bellona is mentioned as a Titan; however, we have found that Spenser is not bound by the letter of classical mythology, and the spirit of it is certainly not violated here. But it is Helios, or Phœbus, the Sun, who in the classics is most often designated by the name of Titan. Spenser follows this usage, as in *S. C.* Jul. 59. E. K., commenting upon this passage, explains Titan as the sun, and says: "Which story is to be redde in Diodorus Syc. of the hyl Ida; from whence, he sayth, all night time is to bee seene a mightye fire, as if the skye burned, which toward morning beginneth to gather into a rownd forme, and thereof ryseth the sonne, whome the Poetes [see *Fast.* 1. 617] call Titan."

TITHONUS. — F. Q. 1. 2. 7; 1. 11. 51; 3. 3. 20. See Aurora.

TITYUS. — F. Q. 1. 5. 35; V. G. 48.

Both of these passages refer to the form of punishment inflicted upon Tityus: a vulture fed upon his liver, which was never consumed, but constantly renewed. The second passage hints at the crime of which Tityus was guilty: he had, for some reason, incurred the displeasure of Latona. *Od.* 11. 576 ff. explains the case in full: "And I saw Tityos, son of renowned Earth, lying on a leveled ground, and he covered nine roods as he lay, and vultures twain beset him, one on either side, and gnawed at his liver, piercing even to the caul, but he drave them not away with his hands. For he had dealt violently with Leto the famous bedfellow of Zeus, as she went up to Pytho through the fair lawns of Panopeus." See also *Æn.* 6. 595; *Met.* 4. 457; 10. 43.

TRIPTOLEMUS. — V. G. 26. See **Ceres.**

TRITON. — F. Q. 3. 4. 33; Co. Cl. 245.

Triton is a sea-divinity. In the first passage he appears as a charioteer, driving his dolphins over the waves; in the second, Spenser calls him, like Proteus, a shepherd, and speaks also of his wreathed horn.

Triton is mentioned by Hesiod (*Theog.* 931) as one of the sons of Neptune and Amphitrite; Virgil (*Æn.* 10. 209 ff.) describes him as of hairy front, displaying a human form down to the waist, and terminating in a 'pristis.' He mentions, also, his shell trumpet, as other writers usually do — among them Ovid, who thus describes it (*Met.* 1. 333 ff.): "The hollow-mouthed trumpet is taken up by him, which grows to a great width from its lowest twist; the trumpet, which, soon as it receives the air in the middle of the sea, fills with its notes the shores lying under either sun." In this typical passage, Triton appears as the attendant of Neptune, whom he usually accompanied.

TRITONIAN (goddess). — Mui. 265.

Authorities differ as to the origin of this name by which Minerva is often called: some say it is from Lake Tritonis in Libya, for, according to Herodotus 1. 180, the nymph of that lake was believed by the Libyans to be the mother of Minerva by Neptune; others say the name is derived from the Cretan word meaning "head," the reference being to the birth of Minerva from the head of Jove, as referred to in *Hom. Hymn to Pallas.* Compare "Tritonia" in *Met.* 2. 783; 5. 270; Claudian, *Gigant.* 91.

TRYPHON. — F. Q. 3. 4. 43; 4. 11. 6.

For Tryphon of sea gods the soveraine leach is hight.

This statement is original with Spenser; for while the name itself was a common one, it is nowhere used by the ancients to designate a mythical surgeon of the divinities of the sea. Among the Tryphons of antiquity, however, was at least one celebrated physician, a fact which may have suggested the name in the connection in which Spenser uses it.

TURNUS.—V. B. 9. See **Latinus.**

TYPHAON.—F. Q. 6. 6. 11; 7. 6. 15; 7. 6. 29.

For Typhaon as father of Orthrus by Echidna (*F. Q.* 5. 10. 10), see **Echidna**.

His blustering character, referred to in *F. Q.* 6. 6. 11, is mentioned by Hesiod, *Theog.* 306 ff.

F. Q. 7. 6. 15; 29 are instances of the confusion of the names Typhoeus and Typhaon, for which see **Typhoeus.**

TYPHOEUS.

In *F. Q.* 3. 7. 47 we learn that Typhoeus was a son of Earth and one of the Titans — or rather Giants (see **Jove**). His belligerent character, also, is hinted at. All this is consistent with *Theog.* 821 ff., and Apoll. 1. 6. 3, where he is described as the son of Tartarus and Gæa — a giant of most blustering aspect, who dared aspire even to usurp the sway of gods and men. Jove, however, met him in single combat, felled him with his thunderbolts, and heaped Mt. Ætna upon him.

It should be noticed that, with Hesiod, Typhoeus and Typhaon are perfectly distinct, while with later authors the names are used interchangeably. (See *F. Q.* 7. 6. 15; 29.)

In *F. Q.* 1. 5. 35 Spenser says that Typhoeus was in the Lower World, stretched upon a gin (an engine of torture). The nearest approach to this in the classics is the statement of Antoninus Liberalis that, after Typhoeus had been given over to Vulcan under Ætna, that god placed his anvils upon his neck.

In *V. B.* 15 a sister of Typhoeus is mentioned; but who is referred to is not evident.

ULYSSES.—V. G. 67; 68.

That Ulysses was the son of Laertes is evident from *Od.* 16. 118 ff.

For his part in the death of Ajax, see **Æacides**; and for the other references to his adventures during and after the Trojan War, see the several headings.

URANUS.—F. Q. 7. 6. 27. See **Titan.**

VENUS.

Under the names of Venus and Cytherea, the goddess of love and beauty is a prominent figure in the mythology of Spenser. She evidently charmed our poet, as she had all others, both of gods and men, from her very birth. *F. Q.* 3. 6. 2 describes how: —

> Jove laught on Venus from his soverayne see,
> And Phœbus with faire beames did her adorne,
> And all the Graces rockt her cradle being borne.

This is but a particularization of the following lines from the minor *Homeric Hymn to Venus:* —

> Graced at all parts, they brought to heaven her graces,
> Whose first sight seen, all fell into embraces;
> Hugged her white hands, saluted, wishing all
> To wear her maiden flower in festival
> Of sacred Hymen, and to lead her home.

The same hymn says that she was born of the sea-foam, as does Hesiod (*Theog.* 197). Spenser (*F. Q.* 4. 12. 2) alludes to this invention of the "antique wisards," and thinks it a wise one.

> For that the seas by her are most augmented,
> Witnesse th' exceeding fry which there are fed,
> And wondrous sholes which may of none be red.

These lines may have been suggested by those from the *Hom. Hymn to Venus:* —

> Through pathless air and boundless ocean's space
> She rules the feathered kind and finny race.

Both poets thus recognize the power of love over all animate nature, as does Ovid (*Fast.* 4. 90 ff.), and Lucretius, when he appropriately invokes this goddess at the beginning of his *De Rerum Natura.* Spenser has translated this invocation (*F. Q.* 4. 10. 44), where, in the temple of Venus, a tormented lover addresses the goddess. This is but a part of a long passage, which describes the temple of Venus, the aspect and dress of the goddess, and the character of her attendants. As a whole, this passage, while marked by originality, shows a judicious assimilation of the ancients.

Thus the description of the inmost temple (4. 10. 37 ff.) is evidently an amplification of *Æn.* 1. 415 ff.: "She herself in mid air departs to Paphos, and glad of heart revisits her own shrines, where is a temple in her honour, and where a hundred altars smoke with Sabæan frankincense, breathing with the fragrance of garlands ever fresh."

We know from the *Hero and Leander* of Musæus that the priests of Venus were damsels, for Hero herself was such a one; but the linen garb which Spenser assigns them (*F. Q.* 4. 10. 38) was probably suggested by that of the priests of Isis (see **Isis**), between whom and Venus there is a certain similarity, although it does not appear that they were identified by the ancients. And again in 4. 10. 41, Spenser seems to have Isis in mind when he describes the image of Venus as veiled. It should be noticed that Spenser makes a mistake in saying that the statue with which the young man fell in love was the work of Phidias: it was executed by Praxiteles rather (see Lucian *Imag.* 15 and 16).

In 4. 10. 42 Venus is described as accompanied by little loves, etc.: with which passage compare Horace *Carm.* 1. 2: —

> Sive tu mavis, Erycina ridens,
> Quam Jocus circum volat et Cupido.

The love of Scudamour for Amoret, the priestess of Venus, his speech, etc., were evidently suggested by the *Hero and Leander* of Musæus.

Throughout the whole passage Venus is the goddess of love and beauty, as also in *F. Q.* 1. 1. 48; *T. M.* 397; *Pro.* 96; *H. B.*

The well-known story of the triumph of Venus in receiving the apple from the hands of Paris as a recognition of her surpassing beauty, and her bestowal upon Paris of the "fayrest dame," as a reward for his judgment, is referred to in *F. Q.* 2. 7. 55; 3. 9. 34. If lines 23–30 of *Il.* 24 are genuine, they furnish the earliest mention of the judgment of Paris, a myth which became a favorite with the ancients. Hyg. *Fab.* 92 furnishes a clear statement of the judgment and its reward.

Various ones among gods and men were honored with the love of Venus. Among these was Vulcan, whose wife she became, and who, Spenser says, made for her the famous girdle (*F. Q.* 4. 5. 3 ff.). See **Vulcan**.

Her husband's skill was further exhibited by the snare which he made for betraying the love of Mars and Venus. This affair is related at some length in *Od.* 8. 266 ff., and is referred to by Spenser in *F. Q.* 2. 6. 35; 3. 11. 44.

The affection of the goddess for Adonis is mentioned in *F. Q.* 3. 1. 34; 3. 6. 46, for which see **Adonis**.

But her love was not confined to immortals only: Anchises, a mortal, became by her the father of Æneas (*F. Q.* 3. 9. 41). The *Hom. Hymn to Venus* dwells upon their union; and the brooding care of Venus for her son is one of the beauties of the Æneid.

It is by the grace of Venus that hearts are united in wedlock. Zeus enjoins this office upon her (*Il.* 5. 429), and in *V. G.* 61 we read that it was through the favor of this goddess that Peleus and Telamon were "renown'd in choyce of happie marriage." The same idea is expressed in *H. L.* 284: "With Hercules and Hebe, and the rest Of Venus dearlings, through her bountie blest." See **Hebe**.

There are many references to Venus as the mother of Cupid, the god of love: *F. Q.* 1. Int. 3; 4. Int. 5; 4. 12. 13; 6. 7. 37; *Mui.* 98; *Co. Cl.* 801 ff.; *Pro.* 96: *Epigrams* 1. 3. 4; *H. L. passim.* See **Cupid**.

The later poets extended the number of loves: Horace (*Carm.* 4. 1) addresses Venus as the mother of sweet loves, and Spenser expresses the same idea in *Ep.* 364.

For the story of the search of Venus for Cupid related in *F. Q.* 3. 6. 11 ff., see **Cupid**.

For Venus as the mother of the Graces (*T. M.* 403) and as attended by them (*F. Q.* 6. 10. 9; 6. 10. 15; 6. 10. 21; *Ep.* 108), see **Graces**.

Spenser is true to classical mythology when, in *Pro.* 63, he speaks of the swans "Which through the Skie draw Venus silver Teeme." Horace (*Carm.* 4. 1) mentions the "bright swans" of the goddess, and Ovid (*Met.* 10. 708) pictures Venus as harnessing her swans and winging her way through the air.

Although Venus is the laughter-loving goddess (compare *F. Q.* 1. 6. 16 with *Il.* 5. 375), yet upon occasion she can give way to anger and jealousy. The story of her treatment of Psyche is touched upon in *F. Q.* 3. 6. 50; *Mui.* 131, for which see **Psyche**.

Spenser further uses the story as a suggestion for an original myth, in which Venus is represented as angry with the nymph Asteria, whom she transforms to a butterfly (*Mui.* 113 ff.).

Various flowers were sacred to the goddess of love — among them the rose, which Spenser says was white before it was dyed with the blood of Venus (*Daph.* 109), an idea suggested by Bion *Idyl.* 1 or *Anth. Lat.* 85; 366. Natalis Comes, also, tells the following story: "Mars was in love with Venus, while Venus cared only for Adonis. The god of war thought that if Adonis were not in the way, he could win the love of Venus to himself; accordingly, he sent a boar to kill Adonis. Venus, hastening to bear help to the beloved youth, was wounded in the foot with the thorn of a rose, and from that time the rose, which had been white, was dyed red with her blood."

Certain haunts of Venus are mentioned in *F. Q.* 2. 8. 6; 3. 6. 29; 4. 5. 6; 6. 10. 9 — among them the Idæan hill. This refers to Mt. Idalion in Cyprus, on which were "Idalia's lofty groves," sacred to Venus. (See *Æn.* 1. 681.) The "Cytheron hill" of the second passage is a mistake: it should be the island of Cythera, where, according to *Theog.* 192, Venus landed after her birth from the sea, and from which she is called by the ancients "Cytherea" (Hor. *Carm.* 1. 4). With the third passage compare *Æn.* 1. 720, where Venus is referred to as Cupid's Acidalian mother. Paphos is mentioned as one of her haunts in *Æn.* 1. 415. At Cnidus in Caria she had several temples, and the place was a favorite with her (Hor. *Carm.* 1. 30; 3. 28).

The planet of Venus is mentioned in *F. Q.* 7. 7. 51; *S. C.* Dec. 60. 84; *Daph.* 483; *Ast.* 56.

There are further references to her bower (*T. M.* 362); to her chain (*F. Q.* 1. 2. 4); to her sting (*F. Q.* 2. 12. 39); to her looking-glass (*F. Q.* 3. 1. 8); and to certain representations of the goddess (*Ver.* 17; *H. H. B.* 212).

VESPER. — F. Q. 7. 6. 9; V. G. 40. See Hesperus.

VESTA. — F. Q. 7. 7. 26.

Spenser declares Vesta to be the goddess of ethereal fire, in distinction from Vulcan, the god "of this with us so usuall." "Ethereal" is here used in the sense of "celestial," "spiritual," and the line, therefore, means that Vesta was the goddess of consecrated, holy fire, while Vulcan was the divinity of fire in its ordinary, practical uses; and this is consistent with classical authority.

The origin of the name Vesta (Greek Hestia) from ἑστία, a *hearth*, reveals the fact that she was the divinity of the hearth. We know from Ovid *Fast.* 6. 305 ff., as well as from other authorities, that the hearth was the center of the life of the home — a sacred spot: "Before the hearths," says Ovid, "it was the custom formerly to sit together on long benches, and to believe that the gods were there at the board." In both Greece and Rome the idea was extended, and there were public hearths, or sanctuaries of Vesta. The Romans believed that the sacred flame of Vesta had been brought from Troy (*Æn.* 2. 296). It was considered to be the symbol of the goddess herself, and was kept continually burning in the temple of Vesta. Ovid (*Fast.* 6. 295 ff.) says: "Long did I, in my simplicity, imagine that there were statues of Vesta, but afterwards ascertained that there were none under her concave dome. The fire that has never been extinguished lies hidden in that temple."

VULCAN.

The Roman Vulcan was identified with the Greek Hephæstus: he was, as Spenser says, the sovereign of the fire "with us so usuall" (*F. Q.* 7. 7. 26), that is, of fire as a means in manufactures. Thus does he appear in the works of Homer as the artificer of the gods. *Iliad* 18. 369 ff. may be referred to as a typical passage, describing, as it does, the Olympic workshop of Vulcan, with anvil, bellows, etc. Here he made the celebrated armor of Archilles, also described, as well as other wonderful works. Cf. *Æn.* 8. 407 ff. See *Mui.* 63.

Later authors, however, place his workshop on earth, in various volcanic regions: thus, Spenser says in *F. Q.* 4. 5. 4 that it was on Lemnos that Vulcan wrought the girdle of Venus. This is quite classical, since Homer (*Od.* 8. 283) says that island was a favorite with him, and others place his workshop there. The reason for this may be found in *Il.* 1. 593: it was on Lemnos that Vulcan fell when he was thrown from heaven, and the people of that island then received him kindly.

Since, according to Homer (*Il.* 14. 214 ff.), the cestus of Venus was a piece of embroidery, Spenser is not consistent with the classics in speaking of it as wrought with fire by Vulcan. That Vulcan was the husband of Venus appears from *Od.* 8. 266 ff. — the passage describing the means by which Vulcan assured himself of the unfaithfulness of Venus. It is possible that the net described there may have suggested to Spenser the girdle of Venus as the work of Vulcan.

In *F. Q.* 2. 7. 36; 3. 9. 19; *V. G.* 66, Vulcan is used for fire itself, with which compare *Met.* 7. 104, and many other passages.

ZEPHYRUS. — F. Q. 2. 5. 29; Pro. 2.

In these passages Spenser personifies the gentle west wind, after the manner of the ancients. See *Fast.* 5. 201 ff.

INDEX OF AUTHORITIES.

This Index is intended to assist students in discovering Spenser's indebtedness to individual authors.

ACUSILAUS: Founders of Nations.
ÆSCHYLUS: Prometheus.
ANACREON: Lyæus.
ANGELUS POLITIANUS: Cupid.
ANTHOLOGIA LATINA:
    Fates.   Muses.
    Lyaeus.   Venus.
ANTIMACHUS: Graces.
ANTONINUS LIBERALIS:
    Hylas.   Typhoeus.
APOLLODORUS:
    Adonis.   Hebe.
    Ægina.   Helle.
    Alcmena.   Hercules.
    Amphion.   Hesione.
    Andromeda.   Hydra.
    Antiope.   Hyperion.
    Apollo.   Iphimedia.
    Argo.   Jove.
    Argus.   Leda.
    Asteria.   Linus.
    Atalanta.   Medusa.
    Bacchus.   Nereids.
    Bellona.   Œnone.
    Cadmus.   Orion.
    Danae.   Pasiphae.
    Erichthonian (tower). Peleus.
    Erigone.   Sea-Gods.
    Europa.   Talus.
    Eurytion.   Typhoeus.
    Founders of Nations.
APOLLONIUS RHODIUS:
    Amphion.   Erigone.
    Argonautic Expe-   Hecate.
        dition.   Juno.
    Clæno.   Sea-Gods.

APULEIUS: Psyche.
ARATUS: Astræa.
ARISTÆNETUS: Acontius.
ARISTOPHANES: Adonis.
BION: Adonis. Venus.
BOCCACCIO: Graces.
CALLIMACHUS:
    Ceres.   Hercules.   Jove.
CATULLUS: Hymen. Peleus.
CENTURY DICTIONARY:
    Neptune.
CHILD: Phao.
CICERO: Fates.
CLAUDIAN:
    Jove.   Semiramis.
    Proserpina. Tritonian (goddess).
CTESIAS: Semiramis.
DARES: Amazon.
DIODORUS SICULUS:
    Æolus.   Linus.
    Arne.   Mercury.
    Atlas.   Ninus.
    Bacchus.   Penthesilea.
    Founders of   Procrustes.
        Nations.   Pythias.
    Hercules.   Semiramis.
    Hydra.   Theseus.
    Hyperion.   Titan.
    Jove.
EURIPIDES:
    Alcestis.   Inachus.
    Apollo.   Mænades.
    Cassiopea.   Nemesis.
    Cupid.   Orestes.
    Hippolytus.

FULGENTIUS:
  Prometheus. Thetis.

HERODOTUS: Tritonian (goddess).

HESIOD:
  Amphitrite.   Jove.
  Apollo.   Litæ.
  Atalanta.   Muses.
  Ate.   Nereids.
  Cupid.   Nereus.
  Cybele.   Pandora.
  Doris.   Prometheus.
  Echidna.   Saturn.
  Erebus.   Sea-Gods.
  Fates.   Tethys.
  Graces.   Triton.
  Hebe.   Typhaon.
  Hecate.   Typhoeus.
  Hours.   Venus.
  Hyperion.

HOLINSHED: Founders of Nations.

HOMER:
  Achilles.   Juno.
  Adonis.   Litæ.
  Æacides.   Mars.
  Æacus.   Mercury.
  Ægide (shield).   Nepenthe.
  Æolus.   Neptune.
  Agamemnon.   Nereids.
  Apollo.   Orcus.
  Ate.   Orion.
  Atlas.   Penelope.
  Aurora.   Pluto.
  Bacchus.   Podalirius.
  Chimæra.   Priam.
  Cicones.   Proserpina.
  Cimmerians.   Proteus.
  Diana.   Pylian (sire).
  Dolon.   Rhesus.
  Ephialtes.   Scylla.
  Erinnys.   Sea-Gods.
  Graces.   Sisyphus.
  Hebe.   Tantalus.
  Hesperus.   Thetis.
  Hours.   Tityus.
  Inachus.   Ulysses.
  Iphimedia.   Venus.
  Jove.   Vulcan.

HOMERIC HYMNS:
  Amphitrite.   Aurora.
  Apollo.   Bacchus.

HOMERIC HYMNS — *Continued.*
  Cybele.   Muses.
  Diana.   Pan.
  Graces.   Proserpina.
  Hebe.   Tritonian (goddess).
  Jove.
  Mars.   Venus.
  Mercury.

HORACE:
  Apollo.   Muses.
  Atlas.   Nereus.
  Bacchus.   Orcus.
  Graces.   Prometheus.
  Hesperus.   Saturn.
  Inachus.   Venus.
  Jove.

HYGINUS:
  Adonis.   Hector.
  Æacides.   Helle.
  Ægina.   Hesperus.
  Alcmena.   Hydra.
  Andromeda.   Ixion.
  Apollo.   Jove.
  Ariadne.   Mars.
  Astræa.   Mercury.
  Ate.   Orion.
  Cassiopea.   Orpheus.
  Coronis.   Pasiphae.
  Dæmogorgon.   Procrustes.
  Demophoön.   Sthenobœa.
  Diana.   Styx.
  Ephialtes.   Tantalus.
  Erebus.   Venus.
  Europa.
  Founders of Nations.

JORTIN: Dæmogorgon.

JUSTIN: Semiramis.

LACTANTIUS: Dæmogorgon.

LUCAN: Dæmogorgon. Orion.

LUCIAN:
  Alcmena.   Juno.
  Bellona.   Mercury.
  Ixion.   Venus.

LUCRETIUS
  Aurora.   Neptune.
  Jove.   Venus.

INDEX OF AUTHORITIES REFERRED TO.

MACROBIUS:
  Juno.   Ops.
  Maia.   Palici.
  Mars.   Saturn.

MAROT: Cupid.

MARTIAL: Thetis.

MOSCHUS: Cupid.   Europa.

MUSÆUS:
  Graces.   Leander.   Venus.

NATALIS COMES:
  Geryon.   Titan.
  Sea-Gods.   Venus.

ORPHEUS:
  Alcmena.   Cupid.
  Argonautic Expedition.   Jove.

OVID:
  Acontius.   Cyparissus.
  Adonis.   Danae.
  Æacus.   Daphne.
  Ægeria.   Deucalion.
  Ægina.   Diana.
  Æolus.   Erebus.
  Alcmena.   Erigone.
  Andromeda.   Erinnys.
  Antiopa.   Europa.
  Apollo.   Hector.
  Arachne.   Helen.
  Argonautic Expedition.   Helle.
  Argus.   Hercules.
  Ariadne.   Hesione.
  Arion.   Hesperus.
  Arne.   Hippolytus.
  Asteria.   Hyacinthus.
  Atalanta.   Hyperion.
  Atlas.   Ino.
  Aurora.   Iphimedia.
  Bacchus.   Iris.
  Biblis.   Issa.
  Bisaltis.   Itys.
  Cadmus.   Ixion.
  Cerberus.   Janus.
  Ceres.   Jove.
  Chloris.   Juno.
  Cimmerian.   Lapithæ.
  Clymene.   Leda.
  Coronis.   Lucina.
  Cupid.   Mars.
  Cybele.   Medusa.
      Mnemosyne.

OVID—*Continued.*
  Morpheus.   Sea-Gods.
  Myrrha.   Semele.
  Narcissus.   Silvanus.
  Niobe.   Sisyphus.
  Œnone.   Tantalus.
  Orion.   Tethys.
  Orpheus.   Thaumas.
  Pales.   Thracian (maid).
  Pan.   Titan.
  Peleus.   Tityrus.
  Phaeton.   Triton.
  Pholoe.   Tritonian
  Pirithous.   (goddess).
  Podalirius.   Venus.
  Prometheus.   Vesta.
  Saturn.   Vulcan.

PAMPHUS: Graces.

PAUSANIAS:
  Founders of Nations.   Muses.
      Neptune.
  Graces.   Nereids.
  Hercules.   Pegasus.

PHILOSTRATUS: Neptune.

PINDAR:
  Apollo.   Litae.
  Argo.   Pan.

PLATO:
  Achilles.   Helen.
  Adonis.   Muses.
  Apollo.   Talus.
  Cupid.

PLINY: Adonis.

PLUTARCH:
  Isis.   Sea-Gods.   Jove.

PROPERTIUS:
  Cupid.   Founders of Nations.

QUINTUS CALABER: Penthesilea.

SCHOLIAST (Ap. Rh.): Erigone.

SCHOLIAST (Statius): Dæmogorgon.

SCHOLIAST (Theoc.): Pan.

SENECA: Graces.   Hippolytus.

SERVIUS:
  Atlas.   Nyctelius.
  Cupid.   Orion.
  Cybele.   Penthesilea.
  Demophoön.   Titan.
  Hercules.

SOPHOCLES:
  Cassiopea.   Nemesis.
SPOLETINUS: Sea-Gods.
STATIUS:
  Apollo.   Muses.
  Dæmogorgon.   Pegasus.
  Founders of   Thetis.
    Nations.
STRABO:
  Founders of   Sea-Gods.
    Nations.   Thracian (maid).
  Neptune.
TACITUS: Flora.
THEOCRITUS:
  Adonis.   Diana.
  Cupid.   Pan.
THEODONTIUS: Graces.
TZETZES:
  Deucalion.   Jove.
  Founders of   Œnone.
    Nations.
VIRGIL:
  Acheron.   Æneas.
  Achilles.   Amazon.
  Ægide (shield).   Atlas.
  Æolus.   Aurora.

VIRGIL — *Continued.*
  Avernus.   Lethe.
  Bellona.   Linus.
  Boreas.   Megæra.
  Brontes.   Mercury.
  Camilla.   Minos.
  Celæno.   Morpheus.
  Cerberus.   Muses.
  Charon.   Myrrha.
  Chimæra.   Neptune.
  Cocytus.   Orpheus.
  Cupid.   Pan.
  Cyparissus.   Phlegethon.
  Diana.   Pluto.
  Dryope.   Priam.
  Elysian.   Proserpina.
  Erebus.   Proteus.
  Erinnys.   Scylla.
  Hecate.   Sea-Gods.
  Helen.   Silvanus.
  Hercules.   Styx.
  Hippolytus.   Tartarus.
  Hydra.   Theseus.
  Inachus.   Tisiphone.
  Iris.   Tityus.
  Ixion.   Triton.
  Juno.   Venus.
  Latinus.   Vesta.

www.ingramcontent.com/pod-product-compliance
Lightning Source LLC
Chambersburg PA
CBHW021939160426
43195CB00011B/1151